A Confidential Agent, Volume 1

Anonymous

A

CONFIDENTIAL AGENT

VOL. II.

'Well, Miss Amy, I will not deceive you.'

A

CONFIDENTIAL AGENT

BY

JAMES PAYN

AUTHOR OF

'BY PROXY' 'UNDER ONE ROOF' 'WALTER'S WORD' 'HIGH SPIRITS' ETC.

IN THREE VOLUMES

VOL. II.

London

CHATTO & WINDUS, PICCADILLY

1880

LONDON : PRINTED BY
SPOTTISWOODE AND CO., NEW-STREET SQUARE
AND PARLIAMENT STREET

CONTENTS

OF

THE SECOND VOLUME.

CHAP.		PAGE
XVII.	THE VIGIL	1
XVIII.	EARLY MORNING	15
XIX.	AMY'S QUEST	31
XX.	MR. SIGNET'S PHILOSOPHY	45
XXI.	MR. GEORGE BRAIL	61
XXII.	A DIFFERENCE OF OPINION	72
XXIII.	A SELF-SACRIFICING RESOLUTION	89
XXIV.	MISTRESS AND MAID	104
XXV.	AN ADMISSION	117
XXVI.	PUBLICITY	132
XXVII.	A SUPERFLUOUS PRECAUTION	159
XXVIII.	A TRAITRESS IN THE CAMP	176
XXIX.	WRITING FOR THE PRESS	197
XXX.	AN INTERVIEW WITH THE LADIES	211
XXXI.	UNCLE STEPHEN'S VIEW	233
XXXII.	MR. SIGNET HAS A BAD QUARTER OF AN HOUR	252
XXXIII.	TROUBLE IN THE MEWS	270
XXXIV.	ANOTHER DESERTER	289
XXXV.	THE POSTHUMOUS LETTER	303

ILLUSTRATIONS

TO VOL. II.

'WELL, MISS AMY, I WILL NOT DECEIVE YOU' *Frontispiece*

'THIS IS THE FIRST I HAVE HEARD OF IT' *to face p.* 122

'YOU HAVE COME TO GIVE US SOME INFOR-
MATION?' . . . . „ 184

WHAT DID A CABMAN WANT WITH A PISTOL? „ 286

A CONFIDENTIAL AGENT.

CHAPTER XVII.

THE VIGIL.

IT is five o'clock in the wild winter morning, and Matthew Helston has not yet returned home. The thing had happened once before, and only once; but that it *had* happened is a source of inexpressible comfort to Sabey as she lies awake and listens in the darkness for the wheels of his cab. She hears, however, nothing save the fitful rushes of the wind, and between them the monotonous beat of the small timepiece on the mantelpiece, and the gentle breathing of the infant on her arm. It is weary work this lying awake and listening, even when we are sure that what we wait for will surely come at last; but if we are not sure, if every moment renders us more anxious and less sure, then indeed is it weary—and wearing. By the time the little clock had struck the half-hour with harsh pitiless click, Sabey is in a fever of fret and worry. He has never yet been so late as *this*. To lie any longer inactive and a prey to nameless terrors is now a torture beyond her powers to bear; so she gently rises, taking the most careful pains even in that moment of suspense and dread—for it has come to *that*—not to wake the sleeping babe. Good Heaven! what *could* have kept him? In winter, as a rule, balls do not last so long as in summer-time; and even if Lady Pargiter had tarried to the last, and got home at four, Matthew should have arrived by this time. Even now, however, with her usual thoughtfulness for others, Sabey forbears to communicate her fears to her sister, whose bedroom is on the floor above and, wrapping her dressing-

gown around her, creeps downstairs softly
into the dining room. She entertains the
glimmer of a hope that her own clock may
be wrong—have gained an hour or so in the
night—and that the one in the parlour, regu-
lated by Uncle Stephen himself, and a pattern of punctuality, will show her that she is
mistaken in the time. The pattern of punctuality points to twenty minutes to six, and
her sinking heart grows sick within her.

What a night it is for him to have been
out so long in, and with that cold upon his
chest! And how ill he will be, poor fellow!
That is her best thought. What she thinks
more frequently, but dare not dwell upon, is
that 'something dreadful' has happened to
him in connection with the diamonds. She
knew that he always carried a revolver with
him on such expeditions; but thieves might
carry them likewise, or that very instrument
of his defence might have been wrenched
from his grasp and used against him. If
anything serious had happened John Rutherford would, of course, have come to the

Grove with tidings of it, *if he could*; but he, perhaps, had shared his employer's fate.

Standing at the parlour-window, on the ground-floor, from which she had put aside the shutters, she stared out into the blank dark street, ever and anon passing her hand across her forehead, as though to sweep away from her brain these thoughts, too terrible surely to be realised, or even to be born of sober reason. Without a thought of self, she pictured herself a widow, and the little one above stairs, for whose cry she was mechanically listening throughout this agony, as an orphan. And then again she would upbraid herself for having so little faith in the goodness of God as to entertain such ideas.

Similar calamities, however, happen, and happen every day; and similar hours of unspeakable anxiety and woe are spent by thousands of the frailest and the most innocent of His creatures. With or without cause, they are equally wretched while they last; and well is it for those who can do more than 'faintly trust the larger hope' that hereafter there will be amplest compensation for them. Though but half-clad and straight from her warm bed, Sabey did not feel the intense cold that on the window had set its mark in exquisite crystals; but there was a chill at her heart beyond the power of frost to create, and, alas! with no 'numbed sense to heal' its pain. Thus she stood like a white statue, her face pressed against the pane, but with eyes that burnt with anxious flame strained eastward, till the church clock —its every stroke a knell for her—clanged six.

'He is dead, he is dead!' she murmured hoarsely as the iron notes died away. 'O Matt! dear Matt! I shall never see you more!'

But though she spoke so despairingly, despair had not seized Sabey yet. Matters had, indeed, become very serious. It was no longer possible to suppose that Matthew had merely been delayed by the late hours of Lady Pargiter. But from seriousness to hopelessness is a long step; and after that one bitter cry wrung from her by the sharpness of her woe, she turned from thought to action. She had at least—what many a poor soul has not—friends and counsellors in her wretchedness, albeit incapable of plumbing its depth. It was curious how, during that terrible hour of love's anxiety, thoughts of what people felt and thought about her Matthew had flitted across her brain. Amy loved him, she knew, and perhaps of all people next to herself understood his character; and Uncle Stephen's affection for him was indisputable. But even he, in her view, did not estimate him—his guilelessness, his gentleness, his love of justice, and his unmerited misfortunes and disappointments—as he deserved. Amy and she alone knew the value of that treasure which perchance she had lost. As to outside folks, including even Mr. Barlow himself, she well knew that they altogether failed to understand, and therefore to appreciate, him. His thoughtfulness (not for himself, Heaven knew), his silence born of it, and his reserve, induced by the failure of his expectations, was by them set down to moroseness of disposition; they thought him dissatisfied without cause, and proud, yet destitute of self-reliance. Hints had been openly dropped to this effect, which at the time had only aroused her scorn, but which if uttered now, would, she felt, arouse her hate. There had been no man like her Matthew, nor ever would be, now that he was gone.

For the moment, however, all these thoughts had passed away.

'Amy, dear Amy—something has happened——' she cried, in a broken but far from tearful voice, as she stood beside her sister's pillow.

'Something happened? Not to the child?' exclaimed Amy, roused at once, and leaping from her bed.

'No,' answered Sabey fiercely, for that question had been gall to her. What was the child compared with its father?

'To Matthew.'

'Great Heaven! what? Oh, Sabey!'
Amy did not waste time as she said this:
she was putting on her things—not as Lady
Pargiter did, but with unimaginable quick-
ness—yet all the time regarding her sister
with the keenest sympathy.

'He has not come home, and it is six
o'clock.'

'Is that all, darling? He has been de-
tained, perhaps, by the weather.' She moved
rapidly to the window and looked out.
'See how fast it snows.'

'Snow would not keep him.'

'Nay, but the cab; even John Rutherford's horses are but cab-horses; and if the
horse has broken down they could not get
another, of course. He will be here, presently, depend upon it.'

Sabey had had this hope in her mind
before—for what contingency, good or bad,
had it not entertained?—and had dismissed
it; but such is the wondrous power of
human sympathy, that the repetition of it
from Amy's lips seemed to afford her comfort.

'It is possible, dear Amy, but not probable. He would have come in any case, even on foot, to relieve our anxiety.'

'Of which, dearest, he knew nothing,' put in Amy quickly. 'How *could* he know? He would naturally imagine you to be asleep, as I was—selfish wretch that I am—instead of being awake, as I should have been, to console you. Have you been long up, darling? You feel very cold.' And upon her unresisting and, as it seemed, unconscious frame, she wrapped a second dressing-gown.

'No—yes. I don't know how long—it seems an eternity.'

'My poor Sabey! How shocked Matt will be when he comes to find you have been so troubled about him!'

'Oh, if he would only come!' cried Sabey, dropping into a chair and rocking herself to and fro. 'If he would come, ill or with a broken limb, that I might tend and cure him—if anyhow he would only come!'

'He *will* come, Sabey. Be of good heart. Look, it is getting light, and with the morning, let us hope, he will arrive. It is only reasonable to suppose it, since if——'

'Amy,' cried Sabey, starting up, 'I cannot stand this any longer. I shall go to Paulet Street and learn the worst.'

'The worst! Why take so sad a view of things? It is not like your good sense, Sabey, nor has it sense at all. The place in Paulet Street will not be open.'

'There are always people in the house,' said Sabey, fingering her clothes irresolutely, and with that anxious, listening air upon her face that never left it for an instant.

'Yes, but they will know nothing of Matthew. He has told us what he does, you know; how he lets himself in with his latch-key, and puts the diamonds into the strong room——'

'Ah, the diamonds!' cried Sabey, throwing up her hands. 'They have killed him for the diamonds.'

'My dear Sabey, *who* have killed him?

How can you—*can* you distress yourself with such monstrous thoughts? Have they killed John Rutherford also, then? And if so, do you think we should not have heard of such terrible things by this time? I grant that you have cause for anxiety——'

'I am in doubt,' said Sabey as if to herself, and without taking any notice of this appeal, 'whether to go to Paulet Street or to Hybla Mews. It is possible, as you say, that at Mr. Signet's place they may know nothing; but Mrs. Rutherford——'

'There, again, dear,' put in Amy quickly, 'if Sally thought there was anything wrong with her husband, would she not have been here by this time? He has not come home, of course, any more than Matthew, yet *her* mind does not instantly fly to robbery and murder. As to your going out in this weather, it would be perfect madness; and besides, what would Matthew say should he come home and find you gone? But, if it would be the least satisfaction to you, I will go off to the Mews at once, and Uncle

Stephen will, I am sure, go to Paulet Street.'

'Eh? what?—who is talking about me?' cried a wheezy voice below stairs, for the women were still in Amy's room. 'What the deuce is the matter? I have got such a bronchitis, thanks to the poet Æschylus, last night, that I can scarcely speak; but I can still *hear*.'

'Then he can't go,' whispered Sabey. 'Don't ask him, I entreat of you. It won't hurt me—nothing can hurt me so much as doing nothing.'

'Hush! Frank will go, of course,' said Amy. Then raising her voice: 'Poor Sabey is in a most dreadful state about Matthew's not having come home, Mr. Durham.'

'Not come home?' wheezed the old gentleman. 'Why, what time is it?'

'It is nearly six o'clock.'

There was a pause, during which they well understood that Uncle Stephen was looking very serious.

'Oh, that's nothing. It's this infernal

weather. The horse has slipped up, or can't
get along; or " honest John," as you call
him, has taken an overdose of whisky to
keep the cold out. Matthew will be home
by breakfast-time, trust him. I'll just put
on my clothes and see about it.'

The two women looked at one another,
far from reassured by Mr. Durham's speech.
The tone in which he spoke, making every
allowance for his bronchitis, seemed to belie
his words. The old gentleman evidently
thought ill of the matter.

'Now, Sabey,' said Amy, with tender
earnestness, ' all you have to do is to remain
here with your child, and hope for the best;
it is your duty to your husband, who would
never forgive us if we suffered you to do
anything rash or come to harm on his account. I will go next door and let Frank
have word that he is wanted immediately.'

'He will never let you go to the Mews,'
sighed Sabey, still with her listening air.
'Hark how the wind blows; and the snow
is falling thicker than ever.'

'*Let* me? There is no one who has the right to prevent me,' answered Amy, lacing up her thickest boots. 'You are my sister, and Matt is my brother, just as though he were my own flesh and blood. To him of all men I owe loving service: I shall not fail him, Sabey.'

She would not fail him: no one who could read faces, and had caught sight of hers, so ready and steady, so tender and true, could doubt of that.

'Heaven bless you!' exclaimed Sabey, throwing her arms about her sister's neck, and bursting for the first time into a passion of tears. 'My darling was always fond of you, Amy.'

'Don't, don't,' cried the other earnestly; 'do not let us unnerve one another. What love can do shall be done for Matt. Only, we will take Frank into counsel first, because he has a good head, and will tell us what is best to be done.'

CHAPTER XVIII.

EARLY MORNING.

IT was creditable to Mr. Frank Barlow that, although a bit of a dandy, or at all events a gentleman somewhat choice and careful in his personal attire, he put in an appearance at No 7 within ten minutes of his receiving Amy's summons. There was a certain smugness and self-satisfaction about him which, on their first acquaintance, and before he began to recognise the young lawyer's good qualities, had set Uncle Stephen somewhat against him; but this characteristic confidence and serenity of mind had now their merits in the eyes of the two sisters, and inspired belief in him. Though he had come so promptly, there was no sign of hurry in his face or manner; if he had come to a 'consultation' about a right of way through the Crescent, he could not have looked more cool and collected, though at the same time there was a tenderness in his tone which would probably have been absent had his only object been to instil confidence in a client.

He listened with attentive sympathy while Amy explained to him, in Sabey's presence, what had happened to alarm her, and then quietly pulled out his watch.

'It is now seven o'clock,' he said. 'In case anything serious—which Heaven forbid!—has really happened to Matthew, we ought to hear of it within the next two hours. That is the usual practice with both the hospitals and the police. I am looking at the affair on its darkest side, for it is far more probable that Matt himself will return home and explain matters with his own lips. What is evident, in any case, is that you ladies must remain at home' (his keen eye had noticed Amy's thick boots, and also perhaps a certain feverish impatience in

Sabey's manner) 'to watch events and act upon them. Promptness is one thing, but no good is ever effected by hurry and aimless effort. For my own part, I will just say a word to Mr. Durham, and then start at once for Paulet Street.'

These words, delivered with all the calm conviction of 'counsel's opinion,' had the best effect; especially, too, as the speaker had volunteered the very service that they would have had him perform.

'My dear Mrs. Helston,' he continued, 'I entreat you not to distress yourself. Something has, of course, occurred to delay your husband; but, out of ten thousand things that may have happened, it is very foolish to fix your thoughts upon the worst.'

Then he went upstairs—for the women had come down to the parlour—and, knocking at Mr. Durham's door, went in and closed it carefully behind him.

'What the deuce do you think has happened, Barlow?' inquired the old gentleman, gasping with anxiety and bronchitis, and also with the unaccustomed speed with which he was putting on his clothes.

'Matt has been robbed, no doubt, or some attempt has been made to rob him,' replied the other in a low tone. 'My objection to these errands of his has always been based upon that ground.'

'I never knew you had an objection: you always advocated his going on with them,' returned Mr. Durham not without irritation.

'Only because I thought his giving them up would prejudice him in the eyes of his employer,' returned Mr. Barlow. 'I always thought it a risk; but most of us have to risk something.'

'You think he has risked his life, then?'

'I am afraid that it has been at least imperilled.'

'He always took his revolver with him,' observed the old man thoughtfully.

'A very imprudent plan, in my opinion, Mr. Durham. What did it matter to him if he *was* robbed of these diamonds?—he is not responsible for them, beyond taking reasonable precautions. To shoot at a thief is something far more than that, and of course provokes the thief to shoot in his turn. However, I am off to Paulet Street, where they will probably know something about it.'

'I must say, Barlow, you seem to take the matter rather coolly.'

'I am sorry you think so, Mr. Durham. I will do as much for Matt as any man, as will be proved, perhaps; but it is necessary to retain one's judgment. Poor Mrs. Helston is on the verge of Heaven knows what—she is in the last stage of alarm and distraction; and Amy is, of course, terribly cut up on her sister's account.'

'I hope and believe she is cut up, as you call it, on Matt's also,' answered Mr. Durham. 'If you imagine that Miss Thurlow has only sympathies for her blood relations, or for the person whom she proposes to marry, you are mistaken, Mr. Barlow.'

Uncle Stephen spoke with heat, nor did

he lose sight of the advice of that great public speaker who recommended that the action should suit the words, and the words the action. He was very indignant that Mr. Barlow should have chosen such a moment to impute imprudence, or any other fault, to Matthew ; and also that he should have imagined the latter was not dear to his sister-in-law for his own sake. Who was this infernal attorney (such was the phrase, I regret to say, by which he indicated his present companion in his own mind), that he should imagine a girl like Amy should forget her best and oldest friend in the dazzling prospect of becoming Mrs. Barlow?

'My dear Mr. Durham, I exceedingly regret that I should have given you any offence,' returned the young lawyer, with feeling. 'If you imagine that I fail in respect—nay, in affection—to any member of this household, you do me wrong. It is too much my way, perhaps, to conceal my feelings——'

' Not at all,' put in Uncle Stephen implacably; 'it is a pity you should ever expose them. You never did like my nephew, sir, and you take this occasion—this of all others, confound you !—to exhibit it.'

Mr. Barlow held up his hands in amazement. He was really innocent of what was imputed to him, only he had thought a judicial manner most appropriate to the situation, and had used it accordingly. His appearance was so genuine and penitent, that Uncle Stephen was touched.

'*Pauca verba*, enough,' he said. 'I dare say you mean well, sir.'

'*Facta, non verba*,' returned the young fellow gravely; 'I hope to prove my good intentions. I am off to Paulet Street, Mr. Durham, and if anything such as we have only too much cause to fear should have happened, I will communicate with you direct.'

Uncle Stephen nodded; he could not trust himself to speak. He well understood what the other meant, and the idea of his having to break the news of some terrible catastrophe to Sabey pained the heart which all its weight of years had not rendered callous.

With a tight, lingering handshake from Mrs. Helston, and one grave kiss—the first she had ever given him in sorrow—from his destined bride, Frank Barlow set out for Mr. Signet's place of business.

Scarcely had the door closed behind him than Amy put on her cloak and bonnet for her expedition to Hybla Mews.

'Dear Amy, how fast it snows!' sighed Sabey. 'Why will you not let me go?'

'Well, dear, *because* it snows so fast, for one thing,' answered her sister cheerfully. 'It would simply kill you to go out this morning; whereas I am as strong as a horse, and used to all weathers.'

'But you will promise me to take the first cab you see, Amy?'

'Of course I will! Not a moment shall be lost.'

'Nay, I was thinking of yourself, darling, I really was,' said Sabey piteously. 'And yet I ought to have known you would have had no thought of self, but only of Matthew.'

'Well, of course you ought. Is not Matthew my brother as well as your husband, and much more than a brother? Did he not offer me a home? Am I not bound to him by every tie of respect and gratitude? You talk of the snow—I would go barefoot in it to serve him.'

'Oh, how I love you, darling, for so loving *him*!' cried Sabey, throwing herself into the other's arms.

'I am glad of that: but I love *you* on your own account. Remember, my dear, whatever happens, that there is always one person in the world, though she is but a woman, whom you can rely upon; whom you can trust to stick to you and yours. Not, of course, but that you have lots of friends.'

'And Matthew?' put in Sabey, with an affrighted air.

'Of course, there is Matthew. I only meant that you would find me useful at a pinch. Now I am off. Nothing will better please me than to find that my little journey has been taken in vain, and Matt at home when I come back—— That's well; here is Uncle Stephen. I know he will look after you, Sabey, while I'm away, and see you do nothing rash.' She spoke with a significance that could not have escaped a much duller man than Mr. Durham.

'I will look after Sabey,' he said, 'till the one who has a better right to do so comes home again.'

No one replied to that, which was a sign how low their hearts had sunk.

'Good-bye, darling — good-bye, Mr. Durham;' and Amy passed lightly out, and closed the door behind her.

'There is none like her—none,' said Sabey tremulously.

'None, since the time of the Flood,' answered Uncle Stephen. 'She is like the dove that flew out of the Ark, and she will bring us back the olive-branch of good tidings, my dear.'

Sabey shook her head, and answered nothing. She felt as if a prop had been taken away from her, even with the aid of which she had been hardly able to stand up.

In the mean time Amy moved swiftly on, less like a dove than a swallow, lightly skimming over the new-fallen snow, though with no circuitous or uncertain course. She knew Hybla Mews well enough, having often visited Sally Rutherford in the company of her sister, when the former had been 'down,' as her husband had expressed it, with the fever. Though Amy had said she was used to such weather, she had never been in such a storm, and on foot, before. After a futile attempt to hold her umbrella up against the fury of the wind, she closed it, and walked on with still quicker steps. Not a soul was to be seen in that wild December morning, much less a cab. Those vehicles were always rare in the neighbourhood of the Grove, and especially so in bad weather when they were most wanted.

After half a mile of rapid travel she found

herself in a broad thoroughfare, looking much broader than usual from its limitless covering of snow, and from the presence, in that white waste, of a single policeman, who stared at Amy very hard, and shook his head; not, we may be sure, in reprobation, but from his utter inability to 'make her out.' What call could a young lady like that have to be out-of-doors on such a morning before the very omnibuses had begun to run? The sight of him turned her thoughts into their darkest channel as respected the fate of Matthew. She had very little doubt, in her own mind, that he had fallen among thieves, whom the report of the value of the treasure entrusted to his keeping had caused to way-lay him. A few hours ago he must have travelled the very road which she was taking, but no harm could then have happened to him; if such an outrage had taken place, it must have been, of course, after he had left Moor Street with the diamonds. Then, for the first time, a thought struck her which for the moment brought her to a standstill—

Could John Rutherford himself have been concerned in this matter?

Sally, his wife, she knew well, and had every confidence in her; but John, she had once heard her father say (and this though she knew he had some liking for the man), was, he feared, 'a bad lot;' a poacher, and a man who took more interest in racing matters than was good for him. Such a person was likely to fall among bad companions who might mould him to their own ends. If Rutherford was in league with such, his silence and their having heard nothing of him—which up to this time had been a source of comfort to Sabey and herself—was indeed only too easily to be accounted for. The more she thought of this, the more the idea oppressed her.

Supposing Rutherford to have been honest, it would have been very difficult for even a gang of thieves to have overpowered both him and his fare; but if dishonest, he might have taken Matthew at a disadvantage and without his revolver. The very notion made

her blood run cold, notwithstanding the speed
which she still kept up; and yet, how unjust
and ungenerous, she reflected the next moment, were these suspicions! The man was
under obligations both to Matthew and her
own family, and had always professed a regard
for them. He had been a little wild in his
youth, but was understood to have long
settled down to an honest calling; and she
knew his good wife had confidence in him.
No; she had no right to entertain such in-
jurious thoughts of the man; and when she
should presently learn that he had not come
home, she would strive not to let them revive
within her. And of course he had not come
home.

Not half-a-dozen people did Amy meet
that morning between the Crescent and Hybla
Mews, but at the corner of the latter stood a
little knot of persons just outside the door of
the public-house. The 'Rising Sun' had
been exceptionally late in getting up that
morning, or, at all events, in dispensing its
rays to customers; and these gentlemen,

protected by the portico from the driving
sleet, were waiting till the house opened for
their morning dram.

'It is shameful!' said one, in a harsh,
grating voice, so loud that Amy must have
heard him as she passed by had she not been
so deep in thought. 'I have been here, on
and off, ever since six o'clock. The night
was so hot——' here there was a shout of
laughter. 'Did I say hot? well, of course, I
meant so cold—that I could not sleep; and
there is nothing like peppermint to warm one.'

'That's truth at all events, if it's the only
one you ever uttered, Dick,' observed another;
'and yet you had enough of drink last night,
one would ha' thought, to last you till breakfast-time.'

'Well, yes,' answered Mr. Dartmoor (for
he it was), in that depreciatory tone we use
when speaking perforce of our own virtuous
acts. 'I was pretty tight, no doubt; but I
went to bed early, and slept like a top, as
Baggett knows, for he pitched into me, at
five o'clock, for snoring; but arter that I

couldn't sleep for the cold, and before six I was out here in hopes of getting a drop of gin and peppermint.'

The facts described were not of vital interest, one would have supposed, even to Mr. Dartmoor himself, yet he dwelt upon them with unwonted distinctness and regard to detail. 'I never woke till five this blessed morning——' He was beginning again, when the door bolts were withdrawn from within, and in rushed the sottish crew—save the speaker himself. His eye had glanced on Amy as she turned down into the Mews, and the circumstance had apparently awakened his curiosity. Instead of following his companions, each already clamouring at the bar for his favourite liquor, he made for the archway which formed the entrance of the Mews, and, concealing himself behind a buttress of it, watched her with eager eyes. Presently he brought his trembling hands together with a smack, and exclaimed, in a tone of exulting malice, 'Begad, I thought so—she's bound for Rutherford's! Now, I would give a pound to hear his story!'

CHAPTER XIX.

AMY'S QUEST.

UNCONSCIOUS of the interest she had awakened in Mr. Richard Dartmoor's breast, and even of that individual's existence, Amy sped down the just-awakening Mews, her presence causing a rubbing of eyes and scratching of heads among the few stablemen who were standing at their doors; which, however, ended in a yawn, and a retirement to the harness-room fire, when she disappeared into Rutherford's house. Sally herself let her in, in a costume that might almost have been a ball-dress, there was so very little of it, and with an astonishment depicted on her round, red face, seldom seen except in masks at Christmas time.

'Why, what in Heaven's name, Miss Thurlow, brings *you* here?' she exclaimed;

'and in a morning like this, too, as would be hard upon a Polar bear?'

'Trouble, Sally; great anxiety and trouble upon my sister's account. Mr. Helston has not come home.'

'Gad a mercy, you don't say so!'

'Yes, I do! of course it has alarmed us very much. But how is it you have had no anxiety upon your own account? We thought that John's being absent also was a good sign, so far as my brother-in-law was concerned; unless, indeed, some accident might have happened to both of them.'

'But John ain't absent, praise be to God! John be here,' exclaimed Mrs. Rutherford.

'John at home! your husband come back! Oh, Sally, what *can* it mean?'

'I don't know, Miss Amy, but I'll soon find out.' She spoke with vehemence, and even anger; but as she placed her foot upon the stairs to ascend them, she paused, and a change came over her honest face.

'What is it?' cried Amy, in a quick low voice, and seizing the other's arm. 'What is it you *fear*, Sally? I adjure you to tell me all.'

'I fear nothing, ma'am; leastways, I fear nothing on John's account. He's as straight as a die; yes, I am sure he is, though he goes more often to the "Sun" than I approve of, and mixes there with folks as can do him no good. Oh, depend upon it, Miss Amy, whatever has happened, my John has clean hands!'

'What do you mean by clean hands, woman?—hands without blood on them?' cried Amy, in intense excitement.

'Lor bless you, miss, don't ye talk like that, or I shall have fits,' sobbed Sally. 'I did have fits when John was brought home inside his cab instead of a-top of it, when he was run over by the 'bus. Don't bring 'em on agin with talking o' blood. No; what I meant was, if aught has happened to them dimonds, my John has no more to do with it than your dear sister's two-months babe. It ain't in his nature to covet another man's goods, far less to steal 'em. Don't be hard

upon him, Miss Amy; you're thinking of that
poaching business down at Latbury; but
that's neither here nor there. Rich folks
and poor folks will never agree about game;
but stealin' is quite a different matter, and as
to them dimonds——'

'Never mind the diamonds!' cried Amy
impatiently. 'I want to know about Matthew——'

'Stand here, then, on the stairs, and you
shall hear all John knows about him from
his own lips,' answered Sally, in a voice that
could not be gainsaid. What she meant was
that she had that trust and confidence in her
husband that Amy herself might judge, from
his own tone and manner, whether he was
guilty or not. A plan which was put in
effect at once in this wise: the door at the
head of the stairs opened directly into the
conjugal chamber, so that to one who stood
on the upper flight every word spoken by
the occupants of the room could be distinctly
heard. To this post of 'vantage Mrs. Rutherford beckoned Amy up, and then proceeded

to rouse her unconscious spouse. 'John, John!'

'Um—ah! what is it, lass?' murmured a thick and sleepy voice.

'What time did you come home last night?'

'What's that to you? Late enough to want some *hextra* sleep this morning. Can't you let a body be?'

'No, I can't, or leastways shan't, till you have answered my question. What time did you come home?'

'Well, about four o'clock, and a most cussed morning it was.'

'But you never took Master Matthew home as usual?'

'Um—ah! well, that's queer; no more I did, now I come to think about it; but how should you know?'

'Never you mind; I do know it. And he ain't come home yet, and it's going on for eight o'clock.'

'Well, let it go. I've answered your question, and that's enuff; just stop your

cackle.   Not another word will I say, s'help
me Bob.'   And John rolled over in his bed
like an indignant porpoise.

' John—John Rutherford!' cried a clear,
firm voice from the stairs without; ' listen
to me. I am Miss Thurlow, whom you
know, and I am come about my dear
brother, Matthew Helston.'

To see John's face as this statement
reached his ears was indeed a picture. If
his wife had flung the tea-kettle, which had
just begun to spit and sputter on the fire, at
his head, and herself after it, he would probably have been considerably less astonished.
His first idea was the inadequateness of his
own appearance and surroundings to the
honour thus unexpectedly conferred upon
him, and he snatched at the garments which
plentifully bestrewed his bed, and drew them
about his neck, as Diana might have seized
her dressing-jacket, anyhow, when surprised
by Actæon.   Only John was infinitely more
surprised than Diana was. His face was
purple from the painful sense of the indeli-

cacy of his position ; and the voice in which he besought his wife, in a moving whisper, to say a few words for him, was absolutely apoplectic.

'If you'll only go a little lower down the stairs, Miss Amy,' said Sally, touched by the embarrassment of her spouse, 'John will put on his clothes in a twinkling, and give you every explanation.'

Accordingly in two minutes John appeared at the head of the stairs in his ordinary in-door apparel, and humbly submitted himself to examination.

'What I have come about, John, is, of course, Mr. Helston's absence. Why is he not come home ?'

'Well, Miss Amy, I will not deceive you ; nor, indeed, is there any call so to do, since there is really nothing much amiss. What I thought was that Master Matthew would ha' come home of himself long afore this hour, or I should have gone to the Grove the first thing and let you know about it; but the fact is, he seemed rather bad last

night—and such a night as it was, too!—
with his cough, and Lady Pargiter she kep
him in Moor Street because of it.'

'Lady Pargiter kept him in Moor Street?'

'Well, yes, Miss Amy; it did rather astonish me, I own, for I should ha' thought
Master Matthew was one to go home in any
case. But it did blow and snow as never
was, and her ladyship asked him to take a
bed for the night—leastways, young Six-foot
said so—and so he stopped.'

'It is incredible!' exclaimed Amy.

'I thought it a rum go, myself, miss,'
assented John.

It was a peculiarity of Amy's never to
fly off at a tangent (as is the habit of her
sex) from any subject, but to sift and winnow
it until she got at firm ground.

'Did Mr. Helston tell you he was ill?'

'No, miss; I only gathered it from his
appearance—he looked ill and pale like—
and from his cough.'

'But would you have noticed all that if
the footman had not told you that my

brother-in-law was going to remain in Moor Street ? '

' Well, I don't think I should, miss.'

It was therefore, it seemed, no sudden or serious attack of illness that had caused Matthew to accept the offer of a hospitality so unexpected, and, as she was well convinced, so unwelcome, as that of Lady Pargiter. John's manner was perfectly honest and straightforward; she had no doubt that he was telling her the truth, and yet the truth was so inconceivable.

' No message was given you as to how long Mr. Helston meant to stay ? ' she continued.

' No, miss; it was snowing heavy at the time, so I didn't ask no questions; and the truth is, I was very glad to be let go straight home myself.'

' You understood, however, that Mr. Helston would return in the morning, when the storm abated, and before our household were up, so that he would not be missed ? '

' Yes, miss, that was just it ; otherwise I

should ha' gone to the Grove and let you know what had happened.'

'I suppose I can have a cab at once?' said Amy, after a moment's reflection: 'not yours, of course, for both horse and man must be tired.'

'I'll call one, miss, from the verander,' answered Mrs. Rutherford, who had been a witness from an upper step to all that passed. Several of the cab-driving inhabitants of the Mews were by this time astir, and the vehicle was procured immediately. 'Now, shall I go with you, Miss Amy?' said Sally. 'It's only just puttin' on my bonnet——'

'No, I thank you,' answered Amy gratefully. 'I shall do very well by myself.' She felt it kind of the good woman, but also that her society would just then be insupportable. A talkative, superficial companion is one of the greatest aggravations to anxiety, and poor Amy was still very anxious: her thoughts of robbery and murder had, it was true, been dispelled, but in their place had come a scarcely less dreadful sense of appre-

hension upon Matthew's account. In his
sane mind, and having the physical ability to
get home, it was incredible that he should
have preferred to remain even for a few
hours in Moor Street. Was it not possible
that his brain, overwrought with recent
anxiety on Sabcy's account, in addition to its
usual burden of care, had suddenly given
way? Throughout her journey to Moor
Street, in reality tardy by reason of the op-
posing wind and snow, but which seemed to
her nervous impatience to last for hours, she
felt as if she was going mad herself.

At last the long, tall street was reached,
looking even more gaunt and grim than
usual through the driving sleet. Though it
was near nine o'clock, not a sign of awaken-
ing life was visible ; the blinds and shutters
were all closed as though each house had
held a tenant recently deceased ; even the
hum of the neighbouring traffic was inau-
dible, hushed by the new-fallen snow.

Though Sir Charles Pargiter's residence
showed no more vitality about it than the

rest, all within it were not sunk in slumber, for the cabman's summons brought one of the 'Six-foots' (as John Rutherford had termed them) to the door with even greater rapidity than was usual during afternoon call-time.

His attire, it is true, was not so complete or spotless as at that period : he was, in fact, in a very dirty undress jacket; and the powder in his hair was what the War Office would have described as 'damaged'—it was evidently the powder of the previous night.

'What is it now?' he inquired in a surly tone, and holding the door open only a very little way.

'I have brought a fare here,' said the cabman, 'as is come to inquire after a Mr. Helston.'

'What, *another*!' cried the footman with cynical mirth. 'Why, I'm blessed if the town ain't gone mad about that man.'

'Is not Mr. Helston here?' inquired Amy, who had now herself left the cab, and made her way up the slippery steps. 'Is he better and gone home, then?'

'If you mean the gent from Mr. Signet's, ma'am, he was here this morning to fetch her ladyship's jewels as usual, but that is all we know about him.'

'What? Did not your mistress ask him to stay on account of the bad weather, and because of his own ill-health?—I have been certainly told so.'

'Then indeed, ma'am, you've been told —well, what certainly ain't the fact.' The footman's face spoke volumes; and what it said was, that, of all the brilliant fictions ever invented, that idea of Lady Pargiter having asked the gent from Signet's to stay the night in Moor Street because he had a cold in his head did the greatest credit to the human imagination.

'But his cabman tells me that he left him here!' exclaimed poor Amy in great distress; which, somehow, the very vulgarity and absurdity of the scene seemed to enhance.

'His *keb*man!' repeated the footman contemptuously; 'kebmen will say anything to oblige their fares; or, for the matter of that, he may have robbed and murdered the gent hisself, and tried to lay it to our door for want of a better—— At all events, Mr. Helston ain't here, ma'am,' he added more kindly, seeing that at his misplaced pleasantry Amy grew deadly pale; 'he came at three o'clock, so my mate the footman tells me, and went away in about half an hour as usual with her ladyship's dimonds; and that's all as we knows about it, I do assure you.'

The man had either learned his lesson so well that his testimony was not to be shaken, or, what seemed much more probable, he was speaking the truth. Amy said no more; but dazed with dismay and terror, and not knowing what to think or what to fear, she hurried back into the cab, and bade the man drive to Paulet Street.

CHAPTER XX.

MR. SIGNET'S PHILOSOPHY.

LIKE one in a nightmare, but without the consciousness that sometimes happens in such cases of its being nothing but a dream—nay, with the consciousness that, although too terrible for reality, reality it was—Amy arrived at Mr. Signet's door. The shutters of the jeweller's shop were not yet unclosed, but no sooner was the bell rung than it brought out no less a person than the proprietor himself. The sight of him after her late talk with comparatively irresponsible or indifferent persons, afforded her a ray of comfort; while, on the other hand, her coming had obviously an agreeable effect on Mr. Signet.

'I am afraid I owe this honour, Miss Thurlow,' he said, 'to a stroke of misfor-

.tune; nevertheless, you are very welcome.'
He held out his hand, which she took mechanically, and followed him into the house.
It was brilliantly lit up with gas, and she
could hear people moving about and talking
together in that state of hushed excitement
which an event that has mystery in it as
well as misfortune is apt to create in even
the best-disciplined households.

'Have you any news of my brother-in-
law?' was Amy's first question.

'None at all, Miss Thurlow; I only know
that he has not been here last night: a special
messenger was despatched to me with that
information; and the diamonds are not in the
safe.'

Then for the first time the terrible significance of their absence—forgotten hitherto
in that of Matthew himself—flashed on Amy's
mind.

'Great heaven, Mr. Signet!' she exclaimed
with fire, 'you don't suppose that Matthew
Helston——'

'No, no, I don't,' put in Mr. Signet

earnestly. 'I have the highest confidence in your brother-in-law's integrity : I feel a conviction that no relative of yours—no one whom you have permitted yourself to love and respect—could act so unworthily.'

Amy's emotion was so extreme that she did not take in the full meaning of his words, but only the general drift of them. That he should be paying her compliments while a catastrophe so overwhelming was hanging over their heads never entered into her mind ; she only perceived that Mr. Signet believed in Matthew, and she felt grateful to him accordingly.

'No one that knows him,' she said, 'could ever doubt him.'

'That is quite my view, Miss Thurlow. Pray come in and let us talk this matter over. This is your brother-in-law's own room, you know.'

He led her into the chamber where Matthew was wont to sit and work among the clocks and birds.

Like the shop into which it opened, it

was just now well lighted up, and had a very brilliant appearance. The glare of light, in such strong contrast with the wintry street she had just left, dazzled Amy's eyes, and as it flashed on the gold and precious stones around her she felt like one in an Arabian tale who suddenly finds himself by malign enchantment imprisoned in a cavern of diamonds and rubies, helpless and well-nigh hopeless.

She had not breakfasted, and was exhausted with the exertions of the morning, and still more with its fret and worry. She was conscious that her mind, so long in a state of tension, had now become unstrung; and here was a man who, though menaced by a terrible pecuniary loss, seemed calm and cool and to have his wits about him: it **was** only natural that she should have confidence in him, and that she should show it.

Mr. Signet noticed her pale face and trembling hands; and, ringing a bell, gave orders for a cup of coffee to be brought, which she gratefully accepted, though the

food which accompanied it she was unable
to touch.

'Of course this matter is a very serious
one—to both of us,' he said, when the colour
had come back into her cheeks a little; 'but
nothing is to be gained by distressing ourselves unnecessarily. A gentleman came from
Cavendish Grove this morning——'

'Yes: Mr. Barlow.'

'Indeed! I did not catch his name,'
returned Mr. Signet carelessly. 'However,
he tells me that Mr. Helston has not come
home; he has certainly not been here; and
I have sent to Lady Pargiter's, in Moor Street,
and her people tell me he left the house—
with the diamonds—about half-past three
this morning: that is all we have to go upon
at present.'

Amy bowed her head: that was indeed
all the news they had of Matthew; little
enough in one sense, but in another how
momentous, how poignant with dreadful
possibilities!

'The first thing to be done—in fact, I

have already done it—is, of course, to give information to the police.'

Amy started as if she had been stung, and the blood rushed to her face.

' The police!' repeated she.

' Well, yes; Mr. Helston's appearance has been described to them as accurately as we could, and is now at every station in the metropolis. If he has come to harm—which Heaven forbid—we shall know it in a few hours. Our next move will be to secure the cabman. Your brother-in-law always employed the same man, I understand—one John Rutherford; and Mr. Barlow promised to let me know at once where he lives.'

' He lives at Hybla Mews, Brompton : I have been there myself this morning.'

' Indeed! You are as prompt, Miss Thurlow, as you are energetic,' said the jeweller admiringly, as he put down the address on paper. ' The man is missing, of course!'

' On the contrary, he came home at his usual time. His story, which I heard from his own lips, is most extraordinary. He says that, the night being a very bad one, and my brother-in-law suffering from a cough and cold, Lady Pargiter had invited him to remain in Moor Street till the morning. He accordingly left him there, and came away.'

'Left him in Moor Street!' exclaimed Mr. Signet, starting to his feet, 'and on her ladyship's invitation! Impossible!'

'Of course, it seems in the highest degree improbable; and when I called in Moor Street, I received the same reply that was given to your messenger: namely, that Matthew had gone away as usual after having accomplished his errand. On the other hand, I am bound to say that Rutherford gave me the impression of one who is speaking the truth.'

'It is just possible,' muttered Mr. Signet, pacing the room with rapid strides; 'everything is possible with a woman of that kind. She wanted the money—that I *know*—and tried to get it out of me. Since she could not effect the sale of her diamonds, she may be trying to make me pay forfeit for them.

Twenty-five thousand pounds! It is shocking, it is terrible.'

'But there is Matthew,' urged Amy piti-fully: 'what has become of Matthew? Oh, Mr. Signet, if you could but have seen his wife's face this morning!'

'To be sure, that is terrible too. But Lady Pargiter can't have murdered him. She would stop short of *that*, I believe. Then, again, her people are not so fond of her that they would risk getting into serious trouble for her sake.'

'What *do* you mean, Mr. Signet? That her servants would not have helped her to put Matthew out of the way?'

'Yes, just that; to kidnap him—a mon-strous supposition, of course; but then, is not everything in this matter monstrous?'

'That is true, Mr. Signet. There is only one thing which we are absolutely certain can never have happened.'

'I am with you there, dear Miss Thurlow. You allude to Mr. Helston's innocence. On that I will lay my life.' He held out his hand, and Amy took it in her own and grasped it eagerly.

'God bless you for saying that, Mr. Signet. My brother-in-law is incapable of wronging a fellow-creature. Every one who knows him knows that; and it is a comfort to me to find that you—his employer—have the same opinion of him.'

'I shall stand by him, my dear Miss Thurlow, never fear.'

This time he took her hand in both his own and pressed it respectfully. She had never thought she could have liked Mr. Signet one-half so much as she did at that moment. Whatever happened, she felt that she would always have a grateful remembrance of his behaviour in that hour of trial.

'And now, my dear young lady,' he continued, 'can you give me any information about your brother-in-law's mode of life— the least hint, however insignificant, may be of value—which may afford some clue to his whereabouts? I need not say that we are speaking together in the strictest confidence.'

'Indeed, Mr. Signet, I have nothing to tell. As you have seen Matthew at our home, so he always is: domestic, simple, somewhat reticent and self-centred, he has not, I do believe, a friend in the wide world —beside yourself—out of his own family circle.'

'Self-centred, you say,' mused Mr. Signet; 'then it is possible that he may have some engrossing thought — some secret trouble weighing on his mind.'

'No, I think not; at least, not now. There was a time, it is true, when his mind was greatly occupied with a certain scientific invention—an application of the atmosphere to purposes of locomotion.'

'Ah, an aeronaut—a visionary!'

'Not at all; the notion, so far as it went, was eminently practical; the locomotive was a road engine. He certainly entertained hopes of its turning out successfully, but of late months he has lost all confidence in it, and made up his mind to the disappointment.'

Mr. Signet shook his head. 'No inventor ever gives up his idea, far less accepts failure with resignation.'

'Matthew is quite unlike other people, Mr. Signet.'

The jeweller shook his head still more. 'No doubt, my dear young lady, this invention has cost your brother-in-law some money?'

'I am sorry to say it has.'

'And his notion probably was,' continued Mr. Signet, 'that if he had more to spend—a good deal more—the invention would have been perfected.'

'I don't know about that,' said Amy. 'Mr. Durham would, I know, have been willing to risk something more——'

'Then, Mr. Helston has borrowed money of his uncle?'

Amy's face flushed to the forehead: she felt that she was indiscreet in thus revealing family matters; and she did not see how her doing so could solve the mystery of Matthew's disappearance.

'I believe Mr. Durham lost some money through his confidence in my brother-in-law's invention; but it was given, and without solicitation: it was not lent.'

'I understand,' said Mr. Signet. Then, after a pause: 'Though to your knowledge Mr. Helston had no intimate friends in town, is it not possible that he might have been introduced, through this invention, to certain acquaintances—less scientific people than himself, but with more knowledge of the world? Have you ever heard him speak of such?'

'No. As a mechanician he was self-taught, and he did not care for the companionship even of those who had tastes similar to his own. He restricted himself, more than any man I ever knew, to the society of his own family; but, oh, Mr. Signet, to them he was so dear, so dear! To my sister, of course,, he was all in all. And it is so terrible to have lost him.'

'No doubt, no doubt, my dear young lady; but he is not lost yet, nor the diamonds either—only missing. Let us hope for the best—— George, is that you?'

Some one had just come into the house, and was passing with heavy tread the parlour door. At the sound of Mr. Signet's voice he knocked and entered; a tall, middle-aged man, very clean-shaven, with a grave but by no means a harsh look.

'This is a gentleman from Scotland Yard; Mr. Brail, Miss Thurlow. Well, George, have you any clue?'

'Nay, sir, how should we? We have not got hold of the string at all yet.'

'True. I can give you something, however. Here is the cabman's address who took Mr. Helston to Moor Street last night; and, according to his own account, left him at Sir Charles Pargiter's house. A most extraordinary statement.'

The gentleman from Scotland Yard gave a pitying smile. 'Well, we shall want *him*, at all events,' he said.

'Do you know anything against the man?'

'John Rutherford,' mused the detective; 'no, not against the name; but of course that's nothing.'

'His wife is a most excellent woman,' put in Amy earnestly, 'and I believe her husband to be an honest man. I hope you are not going to put him in prison without proof.'

'My dear Miss Thurlow,' said the jeweller, ' the arrest of this man is obviously the very first step to be taken. Think of Mr. Helston.'

It was this very reason—that she was thinking of Matthew—that had moved Amy to speak. Would it not distress him, if he were yet alive, that one in whom he had such confidence should be thus disgraced, without due cause, and upon his account? And if he were dead, was it not still more incumbent on her to see that his keen sense of right was respected?

'Cannot some watch be kept, Mr. Signet, over John Rutherford: so that, if guilty, he cannot escape; while on the other hand, if innocent, his good name may not be injured?'

The jeweller looked inquiringly at Mr. Brail, who nodded assent. 'It can be done, no doubt, but it will run to money.'

'No matter: since this lady wishes it; let it be so.'

'Nay, indeed, Mr. Signet——' pleaded Amy.

But he stopped her with a wave of his hand. 'That part of the affair is a mere bagatelle,' he said, 'and not worth speaking about—Mr. Brail and I are now about to confer on the main matter. At a future time, probably very soon, we shall be glad of your advice and assistance; but just at first—my friend George here is very out-spoken, Miss Thurlow—and not knowing Mr. Helston as we do, he might say things to wound you. It is his professional duty to look at what has happened from every point of view.'

'I understand,' said Amy, with an in-voluntary sigh, and rising from her seat. 'I thank you very much, Mr. Signet, for your kindness and consideration. There is nothing for me to do but to go home—though it will not seem like home now.'

The thought of what must needs be happening there, if Matthew had not returned, and now that Mr. Barlow had gone back with such ill tidings, made her heart sink within her. 'You will let us know directly —immediately—that you have any certain news; even if it is bad news—which God forbid—you will let us know?'

'I shall communicate with *you*, Miss Thurlow, in any case,' said Mr. Signet, pressing her hand, and leading her to the door, where the cab was waiting: 'I shall do my best in this matter, you may be very sure, and not only for my own sake. Keep a good heart, and hope for the best.'

The advice was good, and Amy did her best to follow it; but it was very difficult. Her whole soul was by this time darkened with the shadow of a great fear; and yet it was so important that her eyes should be tearless and her voice firm when she came face to face, with her no news, to Sabey!

CHAPTER XXI.

MR. GEORGE BRAIL.

IT was on the whole very creditable to Mr.
Signet's self-restraint that he had shown
himself so calm—nay, almost philosophic, in
Amy Thurlow's presence—under the immense misfortune that seemed to have befallen him. He was naturally a man of
strong nerve, which his habits of business
had rendered stronger; they had accustomed
him to deal with large sums of money, and
to run risks with them. Moreover, his experience had not been of the commonplace
trading sort; there were secrets in his bosom
—not disgraceful ones, but simply the accidents of his calling — which would have
furnished materials for half a dozen writers
of sensational fiction. There were, for example, thousands of pounds' worth of jewels

and ornaments of the precious metals in his respectable establishment of which he could scarcely be said to know whether they were his own or not—for which, at all events, there were no owners, and had not been for half a century. In old times tradesmen's books, like the old parish registers, were kept very loosely. Chance customers would drop in and leave articles of great value to be cleaned or repaired, without taking the trouble—so good was Mr. Star's name in the world of commerce—to make arrangements for their return even by so much as leaving their address ; and at that time it was never asked of them. They gave their names, perhaps, by word of mouth ; and the names were forgotten, and the owners of the names and of the jewels never called for them. They intended to ' look in again,' of course : in a week or a fortnight ; but during that little space death laid them low, or madness took away their memory. The addresses of some of them were found out—for Mr. Star was an honest man—but

the restitution of their property was sometimes impossible : they had no heirs, nor did
anyone know anything about them except
that they had lived and died. Others, again,
had never, perhaps, been the real owners of
these precious wares, and after having left
them they feared to call again, lest the fact
should have been discovered in the mean
time, and they should be confronted with a
Bow Street Runner (as the Mr. Brails of that
date were termed) instead of the conciliatory
features of Mr. Star.

Experience or recollection of these strange
matters without doubt now assisted his surviving partner to keep his head clear, when
this loss of no less a sum than 25,000*l.* first
menaced him that winter's morning. He
had never been what is commonly called a
speculator, but the nature of his calling had
tended in that direction. He was accustomed
to the risk of loss—though not, it is true, of
losses of this magnitude ; and, best of all, he
was of a sanguine disposition, and thought
' All is not lost that's in danger ' one of the

best of proverbs. Moreover, he was genuinely in love with Amy, and his sagacity at once perceived that this misfortune, however ill it might turn out, afforded him an admirable opportunity of ingratiating himself with her. And he had taken full advantage of it. He had (with certain exceptions, which her state of mind had not allowed her to observe) behaved like a 'gentleman in the matter, and also ' like a man.' Instead of bemoaning his lost ducats, after the manner of Shylock, he had evinced sympathy with her in her domestic bereavement, and shown that his heart was not altogether in his gold, as she had, perhaps, been led to imagine. Above all, he had established a confidential relation between himself and Amy, which, he flattered himself, he knew how to improve with occasion.

But all this had cost him no little effort. When the news had reached him that Matthew Helston had not been to Paulet Street that morning (which was known to the people in the house by a certain tell-tale dial, which

Matthew was wont to set at the moment of his departure, so carefully was every contingency in connection with the *parure* arranged for) the shock had been considerable; for, from his knowledge of the man, he knew that something had gone very much amiss to prevent the performance of his duty; and the sight of that empty space in the safe, which should have been occupied by the diamonds, had well-nigh stunned him. Mr. Signet was a 'warm' man, but the loss of 25,000*l.* is calculated to diminish the caloric in most people. And there was no doubt, supposing that the jewels did not turn up, that he would be answerable for them to the whole amount.

As he closed the door upon Amy Thurlow the smile flitted from the jeweller's face and left it very grave. Still, there was nothing despondent or unmanly in it, nor in the tone in which he addressed the detective when he rejoined him in the parlour.

'This is the tightest place, George, we have yet been in,' he said, for Mr. Brail and he had done a good deal of business together in their time. 'The forfeit I shall have to pay, if these jewels are really gone, is something enormous.'

'That is, if your man has taken them,' observed Mr. Brail.

'Or been taken *with* them,' answered the jeweller; 'which it is don't matter a dump: Lady Pargiter takes his receipt, and from that moment, whatever happens, I become responsible.'

'You mean his receipt when he comes away from Moor Street with them?'

'Yes.'

'Are the diamonds so large as to be recognisable out of their setting?'

'I doubt it. There are several very fine ones; but I have a drawing of the whole *parure*, if you would like to see it.'

Mr. Brail nodded indifferently, as much as to say, 'That can wait,' and made certain entries in his pocket-book.

'Now as to Mr. Helston himself, Mr. Signet: what is he like?'

'He is of middle height, and looks of middle age, though he is much younger; has brown curling hair; is of stoutish build—no, it must be that he seems to be so from his slow movements. I remember he told me his weight——'

'Can you let me have his photo?' put in Mr. Brail. 'That will save a world of time.'

'I can get it for you, no doubt,' said Mr. Signet; and he made a mental memorandum that he would apply in person to Miss Amy Thurlow for it. 'It will be copied and distributed, I suppose?' he said.

'Yes, at the police-stations and elsewhere.' Then, perceiving his employer to wince a little (for it had just struck him that it was scarcely a delicate thing to ask Miss Thurlow for a picture of her brother-in-law to be published in the 'Hue and Cry'), he added, 'Not necessarily for the apprehension of the gentleman, of course, but for his personal identification if he turns out to have come to grief.'

'I understand,' said Mr. Signet. 'It is my own firm conviction, George, that this man is innocent.'

He really did think so, as well as having 25,000 reasons to corroborate that opinion.

'Just so, sir,' said Mr. Brail coolly. 'It will be as well, however—will it not?—to watch his house.'

Here was another embarrassment. Under ordinary circumstances Mr. Signet would of course have said 'Yes;' but it was not a chivalrous thing to do to surround the abode of his lady-love with policemen.

'You must take your own way, George, as to details,' he answered curtly.

'You have no sort of suspicion, I conclude, sir, as to any person being in any way connected with this matter?'

It was upon Mr. Signet's lips to mention Lady Pargiter, but her name did not escape them.

Nevertheless, he hesitated, and perhaps Mr. Brail observed it, for he entered something in his note-book, which it is unlikely was a mere poetical idea.

'It may be the faintest breath, you see, sir,' he continued coaxingly, 'and yet worth giving voice to.'

'No, there is no one,' answered the jeweller. Then, after a pause, 'Since you are going to set watches, George, I conclude Moor Street will be under surveillance? The cabman protests, it seems, that he left Mr. Helston there.'

'Sir Charles Pargiter's number is 10, I believe,' said the detective, entering the figures in his book.

Mr. Signet said nothing more upon that point, but he had said quite enough.

'This assistant of yours has been always quiet and regular in his habits since he has been with you, Mr. Signet ?'

'Certainly.'

'And his character at home—do you know anything of that ?'

'I know on the best authority that he has lived a most domestic life.'

'You say " on the best authority," ' said Mr. Brail, with the least quiver of a smile upon his respectable features—'that of his wife, I conclude ?'

'No, not his wife. I have learnt so from his sister-in-law, the young lady who has just left us.'

'I am glad to hear that, Mr. Signet, because a man's wife—I may say it to you, who are a bachelor—is not *always* the person best informed of her husband's goings-on. Indeed, at the bottom of these sort of cases—or in nine cases out of ten of them—there is a woman.'

'Not in this, George. I think you may eliminate that factor from your calculations altogether.'

Mr. Brail's face fell like a barometer before a hurricane. 'I am sorry to hear that, sir,' he said naïvely. 'When women are in any little matter of this kind there is always hope; they are so much more easy to get at than the male kind. However, we must do our best.' And the detective rose and put away his note-book in his breast-pocket.

'My good Brail, you will take your own way, of course; but it strikes me you are entering on this affair under a total misconception,' said the jeweller gravely. 'You must remember that not only the diamonds have disappeared, but this unfortunate Mr. Helston himself.'

'Nay, that is just what I do remember, Mr. Signet. When an inanimate object is missing, we say it cannot have gone without hands—that is, somebody must needs have taken it; but when a man is missing, I say he cannot have gone without legs—that is, he is much more likely to have run away than to have been carried. However, we shall know more about it in a few hours.'

CHAPTER XXII.

A DIFFERENCE OF OPINION.

WHEN misfortune befalls us it is the habit of
many of us to picture it to ourselves as the
worst that can happen; not because we really
believe so, but from a vague superstitious
notion that thereby the worst will be averted
from us. 'Fate has now done all the mischief in her power,' we say. 'It is the last
turn of the rack; whatever happens now
must be an improvement.' It has been the
custom of poor mortals from the earliest
ages thus to attempt to propitiate cruel Fortune. It is no humble submission on our
part, by any means. What we would tell
her if we dared is—'Heaven knows, you
have been hard enough upon us, and too
hard: it is surely time to stay your pitiless
hand.'

On such persons the blow has often fallen, only, alas! to be repeated while the smitten limb is yet tender, and ere the tender wound is healed. But while suspense endures we can use no such language. We dare not say—'Now let Fate do her worst,' while she only menaces us; we cannot reconcile ourselves to a calamity—far less experience 'the low beginnings of content'—until it has absolutely occurred.

'The shadow on the dial proves the passing of the trial,' says the poet—'proves the presence of the sun;' but that is not so with Suspense, which is the presence of the trial, and seems to augur the passing of the sun for evermore. And so it was with Sabey when hour after hour went by and brought her no tidings of her husband.

She was wretched, yet grew more so with every minute of time, which again seemed to bear her on towards an eternity of wretchedness that was to date from the moment she heard for certain—'Matthew is dead.'

Mr. Barlow, of course, brought her no news of him. He had seen Mr. Signet, and been received by that gentleman with a coldness that he did not understand. He himself had not on that occasion used his judicial manner; he had dwelt, on the contrary, upon the alarm and distress of Matthew's wife—perhaps with some vague sense of impressing the jeweller (should that haply have been necessary) with the genuineness of Helston's disappearance. But Mr. Signet had received the tidings with a certain coolness which to Mr. Barlow had had a tinge of suspicion. He had exhibited very little sympathy with the family bereavement, but had dwelt a good deal upon the loss of the jewels.

'As a man of the world, sir, speaking to a man of the world,' he had begun, and the nature of his remarks was such as might have been expected from such an exordium. He had the highest confidence in the integrity of Mr. Barlow's friend, but it must be evident to Mr. Barlow that the coincidence of

Mr. Helston's disappearance with that of 25,000*l.* worth of diamonds was most unfortunate. No doubt all would be explained in a few hours, and the jewels would be found to be safe enough ; but if they were not so found, Mr. Barlow could hardly be astonished if unpleasant things were said.

It had been Mr. Barlow's habit, as we know, to defend Mr. Signet—or at all events to make light of what in his character of employer had seemed disagreeable to his brother-in-law *in posse*; but that visit to Paulet Street had altered his views. As a gentleman learned in the law, albeit 'belonging to the lower branch of the profession,' he felt that he had not been treated with proper respect by the jeweller, though at the same time he was disposed to make great allowances for his position. He did not think that even the risk of losing 25,000*l.*—if he had had it to lose—would in his own case have made him behave with churlishness or irritation; but he admitted that it excused much in Mr. Signet's tone and manner. He remembered that Matthew had been in his employment but a year or two, and that in the case of a catastrophe so tremendous a man was likely to forget all interests but his own, and to thrust forth the *antennæ* of suspicion in all directions. But he left Mr. Signet's establishment with the conviction that the jeweller was by no means certain that Matthew Helston—the man to whose sister-in-law he was engaged to be married—had not absconded with Lady Pargiter's jewels, and he felt great indignation accordingly.

To Sabey, of course, he said not a word of this. It was somehow a comfort to him—not only on her own account—that the idea that such a suspicion could be entertained by anyone had evidently never entered her mind. If she thought of the jewels at all, it was only because the present possessor of them had in all probability been the cause of her husband's misfortune; but what at present monopolised her thought was the misfortune itself, and vague but terrible speculations as to the extent of it.

The explanations of her husband's absence which she had hitherto offered to herself, or which had been suggested by others, were now become impossible. Since Matthew must needs be aware of her anxiety, nothing she well knew could have prevented him— save serious illness or death—from relieving it by this time. One chance only remained after Mr. Barlow's return from Paulet Street: Matthew might have been taken ill, and commissioned Rutherford to inform her of the fact, which the cabman had omitted to do; but it was to Mr. Barlow's credit that he did not encourage this faint spark of hope. He was too upright a man to affect to be sanguine in such a case, or to permit Sabey to purchase a temporary comfort for which she would probably have to pay a high price in subsequent disappointment.

The delay in Amy's return, which seemed hopeful to poor Sabey, rather distressed him than otherwise upon the former's account. He was not pleased to find that she had gone alone on such a morning to such a place as

Hybla Mews; and, though he did not say
so, Sabey perceived it. It would be too much
to say that she resented this—for, had she
not herself entertained the same objections?
But it seemed hard to her that he should
grudge the service which Amy had volunteered for Matthew's sake—the last, perhaps,
that she would ever do for him. There was
already something of the sacredness of death
associated with her husband; and all slight
of him, as well as all depreciation, was sacri-
lege.

'I had rather be alone till Amy comes, if
you please,' said Sabey quietly, almost humbly,
when Mr. Barlow had made his report; and
her face was already turned to the window,
with its listening air again, ere he had closed
the parlour-door to join Uncle Stephen, who
had left her to herself, seeing that it was
better so, and retired to the smoking-room.

There was plenty of movement now in
Cavendish Grove: men hurried Citywards
with heads bowed down to meet the driving
snow; the light carts of the tradesmen flitted

noiselessly by, and now and then a luggage-laden cab from the railway-station, full of the happy faces of schoolboys, bound for home and holidays. How strange it seemed to her that people should go about their business or their pleasure while her heart was gnawed with such a cruel care!

How keen its tooth was, and how incessant was the pain!

Presently a cab drove up with Amy in it; she caught sight of her pale sad face and read its tidings in an instant.

'You have no news of Matthew?' were her first words.

'No, dear, none,' answered Amy, as she embraced her sister in the little hall.

'But your no news is not good news?'

'No, it is not. Still, dear Sabey, it is not bad: not necessarily bad. Only sad and strange, and indeed inexplicable.'

Then, as they sat close together in the parlour, she told her what had happened: of her visit to the cabman, and how Rutherford had told her that Lady Pargiter had invited Matthew to remain in Moor Street.

'That is false!' cried Sabey, just as Amy herself had cried. 'She is a woman without a heart.' She said this with unconscious vehemence, using a phrase of Matthew's own with reference to her ladyship. 'What does she care for what has happened to my darling, so long as her diamonds are safe?'

'But her diamonds are not safe, Sabey. Her servants say that Matthew left the house with the jewels as usual, whereas Rutherford avers——'

'I believe Rutherford,' interrupted Sabey quickly. 'Matt always had confidence in Rutherford.'

Amy knew not what to answer to this illogical remark; moreover, she was in doubt upon the point herself; so she went on with her recital.

Sabey hung upon her words, yet always with ear and eye expectant for that which did not come—of that of which, when all was told, there seemed to be no hope of the coming. At the end she made no observation, but her shapely head drooped a little, and her fingers clasped one another over her lap.

'You must not despair, dearest,' whispered Amy. 'If anything dreadful—that is, very dreadful—had happened, it must needs have been known by this time. Everything will be done that can be done : not only by us, but by others more powerful. Mr. Signet will not leave a stone unturned.'

'God bless him—God in Heaven bless him!' murmured Sabey.

Amy had not the heart to say what she had in her mind, that it was the loss of the diamonds which would set so many shoulders to the wheel—and Mr. Signet's among them —rather than the calamity which had happened to Matthew himself. Yet she thought Mr. Signet had been very kind.

'We must have patience, Sabey, and for Matthew's sake—as Mr. Signet says, it is so all-important to keep a good heart.'

To this too—as to 'vacant chaff well

meant for grain'—Sabey answered nothing, but took the hand that Amy laid on hers and pressed it.   Breakfast she could not touch, though at Amy's request—and with the old argument to back it, namely, that so Matthew would have had it—she strove to do so.

'Presently, my dear,' she said, with a pitiful smile ; but in truth it seemed to her that she would never eat again.

There are some people to whom, like her, taste and appetite are denied; who eat to live, or say so; but to her even this excuse for a meal was wanting.   'What had she now to live for?' was the question she put to herself, when, as if in answer to it, the babe above stairs began to wail.

Sabey rose at once.   'Frank is here, darling, with Uncle Stephen.   You will see him while I go to baby.'

It was not Sabey's habit to call Mr. Barlow Frank, but she did so now to please her sister, and also because she felt that there was a grain of bitterness in her feelings towards him, and that she therefore owed him compensation.

There are some natures which no stress or strain of personal misery can ever warp from being just to others.

Amy found Frank and Uncle Stephen smoking the calumet of peace together in more than one sense. The little irritation which the former had aroused in the latter's breast before starting on his errand had quite passed away, or was lost in the gravity of the common danger. For Mr. Barlow had opened his whole mind to his companion as to Matthew's case, which he considered well-nigh desperate.

'Knowing him as we do, Mr. Durham, I can conceive that nothing short of the very worst could have prevented his communicating with us.'

'Do you mean that he has been murdered?' asked the old gentleman bluntly.

'I fear he has fallen into bad hands—yes.'

After which they had smoked without speaking until Amy entered the room.

It struck her that, though both looked very sad and grave, Frank's face had more distress in it—which surprised, though it did not displease her. She did not understand that when we grow very old we have not the same capability for pain. We have seen so much misery in the world, even if we have not ourselves experienced it, that it has no longer that exceptional character which gives it its sharpest sting. To Uncle Stephen poor Sabey was no peculiar victim of Fate's malice, but was only sharing the common lot. His heart bled for her and for his nephew, whom he dearly loved; but there was a certain cynicism, not as regarded them, but the general fitness or unfitness of things, which dulled its pain. When we have not religion to console us, we have often philosophy.

The two men listened to her tale with the utmost interest.

'This man Rutherford knows all about it,' was Mr. Barlow's verdict. 'His story will not hold water for a moment.'

'I don't think you would have said so, Frank, if you had heard him tell it.'

'It seems that everything is being done by Mr. Signet that can be done,' observed Uncle Stephen.

'I really think so,' assented Amy. 'I never saw a man more in earnest, or, under the circumstances, more judicious and self-possessed. The detective to whom he has entrusted the case also seemed very intelligent.'

'He should have got a warrant out and the cabman in custody before this,' said Mr. Barlow.

'He did propose it, but it was I myself who objected to it, Frank. If you had heard Rutherford speak of this matter yourself, you would have been of my opinion; and it is so terrible to put an innocent man in prison. Think what people may say of dear Matt himself, and how shocking it would be even to hear it.'

'And what was Mr. Signet's view?' inquired Mr. Barlow, not without a touch of sarcasm.

'Well, at first he was of the detective's opinion, that the poor man should be thrown into gaol; but afterwards he argued, with me, that it would be an act of injustice. Why do you smile, Frank?'

'At your simplicity, my darling. I think I can get at the back of Mr. Signet's mind in this matter. You imagine he is sorry about Matthew, whom he never liked, and about Sabey, whom he has seen but twice in his life; and not about these diamonds, for the loss of which he is responsible.'

'I do not say that, Frank,' answered Amy, quietly; 'I say that, considering the enormous stake which he himself has in this affair, he showed much feeling for our distress.'

'If the diamonds were found, and not Matthew, however, you would find that he would exhibit considerable equanimity,' observed Mr. Barlow. 'That was my impression, at least, from my interview with him this morning.'

'It was not mine, Frank; and indeed, unless from a kind motive, I don't see why he should have given himself the trouble to express an interest in the matter at all.'

'Of course he feels an interest in Matthew's loss,' replied Mr. Barlow, 'because the diamonds are lost with him. And as to your notion of his having scruples about arresting Rutherford, there is no "kind motive" about it. He wishes to treat him tenderly, as an angler treats his worm——'

'Or a lawyer treats his witness,' put in Uncle Stephen.

'Just so,' assented Mr. Barlow, unconscious of the sarcasm. 'So far as Rutherford's testimony goes—that is, if it is worth anything at all—it tends to prove the diamonds are in Lady Pargiter's possession, and consequently that Mr. Signet is not responsible for them. His object, therefore, is not to make an enemy of the man, but rather to induce him to stick to his text.'

'If the effect of a legal education is to induce such a want of charity as that speech exhibits, Frank,' said Amy, with emphasis, ' then I am glad I am not a lawyer.'

And, with a remark that Sabey had been already left alone too long, she quitted the room.

CHAPTER XXIII.

A SELF-SACRIFICING RESOLUTION.

THOUGH our Dead be in their new-made graves, and our Lost unfound, the wheel of life goes on with us. We sleep (sometimes), and forget our woes; we eat, and are strengthened to bear them. Breakfast and dinner and tea were served as usual in the little household in Cavendish Grove, and partaken of, though sparingly. Uncle Stephen ate and drank his ordinary share, for the appetite of the aged is little affected by mental care; and Amy took what she could, in readiness for whatever demand might be made upon her energies; she had sent word to her pupils to explain her absence from them, which, for Sabey's sake, she was resolved should last till this state of suspense should be terminated. Otherwise she would have hailed her ordinary occupation as an escape from thought.

Her sister forced herself to sit at table, but every morsel she strove to swallow seemed to choke her; directly after meals she went back, like some mechanical figure whose spring is set free, to her seat by the parlour window.

It was twelve hours now since Matthew ought to have arrived at home, and no tidings had come of him, nor any word from Mr. Signet. The snow had ceased, but the mantle of night had fallen, and the wind still wailed and shrieked. Did he hear it, she wondered, and feel the bitter cold, or was he in Heaven? In the latter case, he could not be watching her (as she would have otherwise fondly pictured), for her misery would have made him wretched.

Now and then, she would go upstairs and see for the fortieth time that everything was arranged for her husband's reception in case he should be brought home ill. There was a fire in his room, the flame of which, as it fell upon anything of his, and showed it to her yearning eyes, seemed to scorch her very soul. Mothers who have lost their only children, and look upon their toys, were said to suffer the like; but surely it could scarcely be so. At her own earnest request, she was mostly left alone; but Amy was on the watch for her, with the child.

At four o'clock Mr. Barlow came home from the city, to which he had gone as usual, and was let in by Amy herself.

'Have you any news?' was his eager inquiry.

'No; have not *you*, Frank?'

He shook his head. 'Well, not exactly news, and certainly not good news, but——.'

She laid her finger on her lip; but Sabey, who had run downstairs on hearing the front door open, was already beside them.

'What is it, Frank?' she said. 'I can bear anything but this suspense.'

'It must soon be over, dear Mrs. Helston. What I was going to say was, that the Press had got hold of the affair; so that the mystery, at least, about poor Matthew cannot long remain unexplained.'

'Then, why did you say it was "certainly not good news"?' she inquired with simplicity.

'Well, only that it is not pleasant to find one's private affairs in the newspapers; I had hoped that we should have come to the end of our trouble without publicity.'

'What does it matter, if Matthew is only found?'

'That is true: I am glad, my dear Mrs. Helston, that you take so sensible a view of the matter; I was only afraid it might have been an additional source of distress to you.'

As he said this he glanced significantly at Amy: she understood at once that he was deceiving her sister; and no doubt it was for her good: perhaps something had come to his knowledge which it was essential to keep from Sabey: yet it seemed so cruel to play her false. Her suspicions were so easily lulled, and she had such complete trust in everyone about her. It seemed like abusing the confidence of a child.

'Of course I could not do much good at the office,' said Mr. Barlow.

'It was I who sent you there,' put in Amy: she had indeed insisted on his going, since his presence could have been of no avail at home, and she knew how irksome it would have been to him, for he was a man devoted to his calling; but she wished Sabey to understand how this had been.

'Of course I should have remained here,' said Mr. Barlow, 'could I have been of any service.'

'I am sure you would,' said Sabey gratefully; her ears were open to his words, but her eyes were once more peering through the pane into the darkness without.

'I could do no work, however,' continued Mr. Barlow, 'for my thoughts were with you both. My partner is a shrewd fellow, but I did not like to speak with him about our trouble without consulting you, Mrs. Helston. I clung to the hope that

when I came back all might be well, and
that there might be no need for taking all
the world—or any of it—into our confidence.
I think, however, if nothing occurs in the
mean time, that I will consult with Mr. Bates
to-morrow.'

Sabey answered not a word: when an
acknowledgment of kindness seemed to have
been necessary, she had made it; but nothing
short of such an appeal could now arouse
her attention. What was Mr. Bates to her,
or Mr. Anybody-else?

Amy turned a mournful look upon her
lover, and lifted her hands in pity. 'She
does not hear you, Frank,' she whispered.
'What is it you were going to say to me
when you came in?'

He pulled a newspaper half-way out of
his pocket, and motioned her towards the
door. They rose softly and went out; as
they did so the dining-room door opened,
and Uncle Stephen beckoned them in. It
was pitiful to see what pains the old gentleman took to be very quiet in his own house,

·as though Death—and not the fear of Death —were already in it.

'I knew you had come, Barlow,' he said, 'but thought it better to keep away. The presence of other people seems to add to poor Sabey's burden. What have you heard?'

'Nothing. The thing is not talked about ·as yet, but I have seen something. Here is the evening paper with a paragraph about it.' He pulled it from his pocket and read aloud: "MYSTERIOUS DISAPPEARANCE OF A JEWELLER'S ASSISTANT.—*It is rumoured that the assistant of a well-known jeweller, not a hundred miles from Paulet Street, is* non inventus." '

'What *English* and what Latin!' ejaculated Uncle Stephen, screwing up his face as though he had heard a sharpening of saws: 'pray finish with it.'

" ' *By a coincidence, which is, to say the least, unfortunate, a large amount of valuable diamonds are found to be missing from the same establishment. The Police have been*

communicated with, however, and we under-
stand that they have a clue." The meaning
of that paragraph is plain enough, I think.'

'You are paying it the only compliment
that is possible,' said Uncle Stephen. 'It is
curious how villanous a style of writing may
be acquired by long practice.'

'It is the *suggestio falsi* with a ven-
geance,' observed Mr. Barlow.

('I wonder they didn't put *that* in,' soli-
loquised Uncle Stephen; likewise *propria
quæ maribus* and *as in præsenti.*')

'If Sabey read it, it would break her
heart,' said Amy, with a shudder.

'I hope not,' returned Uncle Stephen,
contemptuously.

'But surely what the man implies is that
Matthew is a thief,' urged Amy.

'Very likely, my dear; but what is the
opinion of such a personage—with his *non
inventus* and his "not a hundred miles from
Paulet Street"—worth?'

'He is a common person, no doubt,' observed Mr. Barlow, 'but that is, in one view,

so much the worse for us. His opinion will be the common opinion. We must make up our minds for that. This is but the first spatter of the mud-shower.'

'Do you really think so, Frank?'

'I am sure of it, Amy.'

'Alas, my poor dear Sabey! as though she had not enough to bear already!'

'That is true,' said Uncle Stephen; 'but I am much mistaken if any vile innuendo against her husband will not act as a counter-irritant. It will be harder to bear, perhaps, but in another sort of way. It is her love that makes her loss so terrible : these calumnies will be armour to herself as much as a weapon to his enemies, for she has plenty of spirit.'

'But how frightful to be thus forced to take up arms!' sighed Amy.

'No doubt,' said Mr. Barlow: 'yet I believe Mr. Durham is right. That the necessity will arise is certain : we shall all have to take up arms. I have given the case my best attention the whole day, and I am convinced that, if poor Matthew does not turn up within a few hours, all the world, with a few exceptions, will be of this penny-a-liner's opinion. We shall be in a minority of four.'

'That is about the proportion of sensible folks to the mass of the population,' observed Uncle Stephen, with a philosophic air. 'Upon my life—with the exception of the present company, of course—I don't *know* four people capable of appreciating a contingent truth.'

'Nothing, at all events, can make our minority less small,' observed Amy. 'Whatever others may think, we shall *know* that Matthew Helston can never be associated with crime or shame.'

'That is well said,' cried Uncle Stephen admiringly. 'If I did not know it before, I should be convinced of it from such loyal lips. None but a true man could have won for himself such a defender. What is your opinion, Mr. Barlow?'

'I think you need scarcely ask it, Mr. Durham,' said the lawyer. 'If I am less demonstrative than some folks in this good cause,' and he laid his hand lovingly on Amy's shoulder, ' you will find me equally devoted to it.'

'Ay, to parody a famous saying,' said Uncle Stephen, with a pucker about his mouth which under other circumstances would have developed into a smile, ' he will go as far in a skin of parchment as anyone in the glittering mail of chivalry.'

'I hope so,' answered the lawyer prudently, not from any distrust of himself, but because he entertained some doubt of the other's meaning. . 'Each must work by his own lights and in his own way.'

'Only let us work together,' said Uncle Stephen drily; 'then we shall stand four-square to every wind that blows.'

Amy looked from one to the other very gravely. It was well, of course, to be assured (though she had never doubted it) that these stout friends were with her and hers; but what she noted with alarm was that they spoke only of defending Matthew's memory, as though they already despaired of seeing him in the flesh.

They had no common meal that evening, for Uncle Stephen's bronchitis was severe, and the two women were glad enough to escape from what was to them but an empty ceremony. Sabey retired early; she had declined, with a grateful caress, her sister's offer to share her bed, but had promised to endeavour to get some sleep. Amy herself was unable to do so, and after a few hours rose and went on tiptoe to Sabey's room. The door was open, the fire burning brightly, and the babe asleep in its cot; but there was no Sabey, nor any sign of her having laid her head on the pillow. What on earth could have become of her? Was it possible that, with a brain half-turned by weariness and anxiety, she had gone forth in the night to seek her Lost One? Half paralysed with terror, Amy ran downstairs, and to her joy found the front door locked as usual; a feeble light shone from the smoking-room below, and with a beating heart, but swift and noiseless step, she descended and pushed open the half-closed door. In the far corner of the room, close to the machine her husband had invented and leaning over it, was Sabey. She had taken the cover off, and was anointing the little wheels with oil and rubbing them with a piece of flannel, just as she had seen Matthew do.

She did not hear her sister's step, but worked on with great intentness. At first Amy feared her reason had given way, but presently perceived that the expression of her eyes was only that of tender solicitude. Did she think that she would have her husband back again, and was thus preparing all things as he would have them for his return? or was it a pious duty paid to the memory of the dead? In either case it was a pitiful sight.

With a gentle sigh, but without disturbing her in her occupation, Amy withdrew as softly as she had come. Her heart-strings were wrung with pity. What a desolate future was in all human probability in store for

yonder gentle creature! What unimaginable
anxiety and woe must needs be consuming
her, which could find relief in such a task as
this! She was almost angry with herself
for having felt such strength and comfort a
while ago from her lover's presence, when
for Sabey there was no protector and no
solace left. Upon her knees that night she
took Heaven to witness that she would never
desert her unhappy sister—never permit the
gratification of her own happiness to interfere with any mitigation of the other's trouble
that it might be in her power to afford. If
it should be Sabey's fate to suffer, and so
undeservedly, then it should be hers to do
what she could to break the bitter stroke of
calamity—no matter at what self-sacrifice.
With her soft eyes turned towards the
Heaven she was importuning for another's
sake, her beauty had a certain ethereal cast
which at other times was not observable;
yet it is doubtful whether, if Mr. Frank Barlow had just then got at 'the back of her
mind,' as he called it, he would have admired

her in this mood so much as in ordinary ones. There are circumstances under which one prefers a woman to an angel, especially if her angelic attributes tend to place one in the position of second fiddle. In this instance, perhaps, that would be to overstate the case. Her Frank was first in Amy's eyes, but he was not all in all; and for the time Matthew and Matthew's wife seemed to have greater— or, at all events, more immediate—claims upon her.

CHAPTER XXIV.

MISTRESS AND MAID.

ON the morning upon which Matthew Helston disappeared from the world of living men, leaving so small a gap—yet one which, for two fond hearts at least, was not to be filled up—Lady Pargiter rose earlier than was her wont after a ball-night. Her face, never at its best in the morning hours, wore a look of care, and she had slept ill. To a close observer—and there was one in the person of her waiting-maid Patty Selwood—she had an anxious air, as though (like poor Sabey) she too watched and waited in expectation of some tidings, not of a pleasant sort. Her tongue was silent, but ever and anon she seemed on the point of speech; while more than once, with an impatient movement of the head, she would look sharply up at Patty (when that damsel's attention was otherwise engaged) with a glance half of distrust, half of inquiry. Once Patty caught her at it in the wardrobe-glass, and noticed that her ladyship turned scarlet and bit her lip, with an expression that showed she was in imagination biting Patty.

How strange it is that, though Civilisation progresses with such giant strides, Human Nature remains much where it was a thousand years ago, or perhaps a million ! If servants had been serfs or vassals, as in the good old times, it is probable that Patty Selwood would have had as hard a time of it with her ladyship as ever had female slave with Roman mistress. It is my belief that she would have put her in the pond that morning to catch lampreys without a twinge of pity. Not, as in the historical case, because she had broken a vase, nor from simple cruelty; but because, for one thing, the girl possessed a secret of hers of the last importance; and for the other, that she kept an obstinate silence upon it to the only person to whom it was safe to speak of it—namely, herself. And she did so long to know if anything had occurred in connection with it.

Under such circumstances it was a treat to watch Miss Selwood's face, who—perfectly conscious of what was expected of her, and resolute not to be the first to speak—exhibited not only the most complete *sang froid,* but a certain innocent gaiety in the performance of her duties, which almost drove the other distracted. She would smooth and smooth anew with the ivory brush the scanty locks of her mistress, as if in ecstasy at their silken softness; and she would set to work again and again upon the slantwise parting (for it was one of the troubles of her ladyship that Nature had given her a tuft on the forehead which necessitated a *détour*), as though it were the one pleasure of her life to guide the plough of tortoiseshell upon that miniature mountain side. At last, as though endurance was no longer possible— ' How stupid you are, Selwood !' Lady Pargiter snapped out; 'you have been more than half an hour doing my hair!'

'Indeed, my lady, I'm very sorry. I suppose it's the damp. What a day it is!— the streets are one mash of snow! And what a night it was! I don't think I ever heard the wind blow so as when you sent after that poor Mr. Helston.'

'Hold your tongue, you fool!' said Lady Pargiter vehemently. 'Did I not tell you never to allude to that matter?'

'Yes, my lady. I ask your pardon for mentioning it again even between ourselves. For my part, I am the last one to blab, especially when so much—will you wear your steel or your silver châtelaine, my lady?—when so very much, as you said last night, might depend upon it.'

Again those prominent upper teeth of Lady Pargiter came out above her under lip, and tore at them with impotent fury. She looked more like a horse than ever, and one that had taken to crib-biting. As she did not speak, however, Miss Selwood continued in her smoothest tone—'As far as I am concerned, my lady, you may depend on it no word shall pass my lips. But as to sending after the person in question, Harvey went hisself, and must therefore know it happened—so far.'

'Is it Harvey's turn in the hall this morning?'

'No, my lady.'

'Not that it matters, of course. Nothing is less likely than that any question should be asked of him. But—what time is it?'

'Half-past ten, my lady.'

'So late!' Lady Pargiter drew a deep breath of relief. 'Ill news flies apace, so it is clear that nothing is known of anything wrong in Paulet Street. We should have heard of it soon enough had it been otherwise.'

'Oh, but we *have* heard, my lady!'

'What?' Lady Pargiter rose from her chair, and turned upon her waiting-maid like a tigress; so fiercely flashed her eyes that Patty with great promptness shifted the chair on which the other had been sitting, so as still to keep it between them. 'Something has happened, then, and you have dared to keep it from me ? '

'Nay, I dared not tell it to you, my lady,' pleaded Patty, with a show of terror that was not wholly genuine. She had had many a sharp insulting word from her mistress, but she was by no means afraid of her. As love in its completeness is incompatible with fear, so is extreme hate ; and Patty hated Lady Pargiter very cordially. It was her *rôle*, however, on this occasion to simulate alarm and submission. 'Did not your ladyship lay express commands on me not to mention the subject, and repeat them to me this very morning ? ' But even while she said the words she could not restrain 'the laughing devil in her eye '—the imp of delight that rejoices in another's pain, while it affects to sympathise with it.

'You lie ! ' cried Lady Pargiter sternly, 'and you know that I know it. You take pleasure in the anxiety which I suffer.' She paused a little, and then went on in low but distinct tones. 'You think you have an easy place here, no doubt, with opportunities for thieving; and you have taken advantage of them. It is convenient, too, to be under the same roof with Harvey. Ah, you '— here the torrent of her wrath was for an instant delayed for an epithet; at last she found one—'you swine ! You thought, because I chose to shut my eyes, that I was blind. I could turn you out to-day without a character, or one that would be worse than none, and into the street. Do you understand ? '

'Oh, I understand, my lady.'

There was something in the girl's voice— a concentration of such exceeding bitterness and malignity—that it arrested Lady Pargiter's fury in mid volley. 'How can you be so foolish, then,' she continued in milder tones, ' to tempt me to such extremities ? I have had an almost sleepless night with thinking of that Helston—" poor Mr. Helston," as you just now called him to annoy me—as you might have guessed by my very

looks. You must have known, too, my anxiety to learn what has happened, Selwood,
and yet you would not open your mouth.
Had I not reason to be angry, then, and to
say things, which, in cold blood, I should
not have said?—-The black silk dress of
which you spoke to me yesterday need not
go to the milliner's; you may have it for
yourself.'

'Thank you, my lady.'

Lady Pargiter was once more seated before the dressing-table, but Patty was busying
herself at the chest of drawers; she could
not trust her face to be read in the mirror
for a moment or two; and it had been no
easy task to reply to her ladyship's generous
offer in quiet, though it must be confessed
far from grateful tones.

'I hate quarrelling with an old servant,'
continued Lady Pargiter; 'and am always
sorry when I have said anything harsh to
her.'

'I am sure you are sorry, my lady,'
answered Patty, in a voice that she did her

best not to render significant. 'I think you said you would wear your steel châtelaine this morning?'

To this, though manifestly intended for her aggravation, as procrastinating the important subject in hand, Lady Pargiter made no reply; she was content to consider it as her waiting-maid's parting-shot, after which there was to be peace between them.

'Well, Patty, and what has happened in Paulet Street?'

'I don't know as to that, my lady; but there have been two messengers here this morning—one from Mr. Signet's place, and one (as I understand) from Mr. Helston's house—to ask what has become of him.'

'What has become of him?' gasped Lady Pargiter like a fifth-rate, or exhausted, echo.

'Yes, my lady; he has disappeared—that's what they say—with your ladyship's jewels; and they came here understanding that Sir Charles had given him shelter for the night.—Take a good draught of the sal volatile, ma'am : a good sniff of the salts. Now you find yourself better, don't you ? '

It was not often that Lady Pargiter 'gave way' except to fits of passion, but for the moment she had been on the verge of a fainting fit. Her face was quite white, save for the tip of her nose, which retained its incandescence. 'I hear from Blake, ma'am, as saw the lady——'

'What lady ? '

'Well, I suppose Mr. Helston's wife ; she came in a cab after the other one, and in a most dreadful twitter. She had a baby, it seems, quite recent——'

'Rubbish !' exclaimed Lady Pargiter ; 'who cares about the woman or her baby either ? All this is only what was to be expected ; I felt it would come, last night. There is a regular plot on foot against me.'

'A plot, my lady ?'

'Of course there is ; they will try to make out that I have got the diamonds— that the man left them with me—don't you understand ?'

'I think I do, my lady.   And what your ladyship wants,' she added with simplicity— 'supposing the diamonds are not found—is to make Mr. Signet pay you 25,000*l.* in place of them?'

'Of course I shall make him pay it.'

'Only, if he knew what *we* know,' observed Miss Selwood, with an air of careless inquiry, 'there would be some difficulty about that?'

'It would cause delay, no doubt,' returned Lady Pargiter, speaking very quietly, but between her closed teeth, and tapping the floor with her foot; 'that is why I enjoin silence upon you—the most absolute silence —and also on Harvey.   See to that at once.'

'But supposing I was asked whether——'

'Hush—be silent; you will not be asked. They will not dare to ask *me*, even.   But if they did, I should deny it.   It is necessary to lie when one has to deal with liars.'

Here there was a knock at the door, which Patty opened a little way.

'There is a man below stairs, my lady, who wishes to speak to you.'

'A man? What man? Not Mr. Signet?'
she added in a fierce whisper.

'No, my lady; a stranger. He says if it
is not convenient he will call again, but that
his business is pressing.'

'Let him wait; I will see him——'
Then, in impatient reference to certain
finishing touches which Patty was giving to
her costume, 'There, that will do; do I look
pale or flurried?'

'You look quite yourself, my lady,'
answered Patty, in a tone that seemed to
imply that was the perfection of feminine appearance.

'You're a good girl, Patty. I was thinking of giving you a little present at Christmas,
but you may as well have it to-day. Here
is a five-pound note.'

'Thank you, my lady.'

'You understand that not a word is to
pass your lips of what took place last night?'

'I quite understand, my lady.'

Lady Pargiter swept out of the room in
her grandest style; a third-rate sort of

haughtiness which reminded one of the minuet just as the tune of a barrel-organ might be suggestive of an oratorio.

Miss Selwood looked on admiringly till the last skirt of her mistress's train had cleared the doorway; then a frown came over her pretty face, and she clenched her little fist. ' "You swine," you called me, did you! And a swine is a pig, I believe. Very well, my lady.'

CHAPTER XXV.

AN ADMISSION.

LADY PARGITER was not a dull woman : she had a great deal of that sort of knowingness which among men is called cunning, and a piercing eye for the main chance ; but she was ignorant in quite an extraordinary degree. Her father, the money-lender, had not given her even the education that women of her class are usually possessed of ; perhaps he felt that she would have money enough to atone for all deficiencies, or, having done without education of any kind himself—and so very well, as he judged—he attached no importance to it. She wrote a good hand—'quite a business hand,' he used proudly to say—and it certainly was not a lady's hand ; but her spelling was infamous. In that branch of polite learning, however, many a

public-school boy is deficient : English litera-
ture and modern history and geography are
ignored in those seminaries ; I met a boy the
other day, who was considered a classical
prodigy and had taken a 'double remove,'
who had never *heard* of Cherbourg. But
then he had the ancient towns of the Peloponnesus at his fingers' ends. Now, Lady
Pargiter knew no more of the Peloponnesus
than she did of Cherbourg. When the public-school boy grows up, he cannot help, any
more than other men, acquiring a certain
amount of general information from newspapers or conversation : while her ladyship
had acquired nothing. She never read anything in the newspapers except the 'Fashion-
able Intelligence,' and her talk was on the
same topic. The philosopher who observed
that everybody could acquire information
who was fool enough to waste his time in so
doing, though it was ten to one that he would
afterwards turn out a bore, has my warmest
admiration. When you once take to improv-
ing your mind, there is no knowing where to

stop; you go through so much to attain so little, that the temptation is enormous to make other people aware of your labours; but to be absolutely ignorant of affairs that are going on about you is to become a nuisance in another way. You are like a person who has a sense deficient, and are a drag upon the social wheel. Before persons of intelligence, who had the honour of Lady Pargiter's acquaintance, addressed her, they had to take precautions to be understood; it was almost as bad as practising the deaf-and-dumb alphabet. The wife of a country squire, whom he had cruelly snatched from a very agreeable metropolitan circle, once informed me that, after many years' experience of Arcadia, she had arrived at the conclusion that not only did her neighbours discuss the same topics, but that they actually said the same things, according to the season of the year; that their remarks recurred as it were in cycles. Being so far apart, and also being destitute of any particular significance, the fact escapes the recognition of the ordinary observer, but that it may be the case is certain from what has been done at whist. In order to fairly try the skill of one pair of partners against another, it has been found necessary to note the hands that are dealt to each, and to give them the same hands—but *vice versâ*—six months afterwards : all recollection of them has by that time been effaced, and they have become practically new.

But Lady Pargiter did not even vary her conversation with the seasons, for she knew only one—namely, the London season. The last ball, and the next one, were her only topics. To listen to any other was a strain upon her attention, and the attention of a lady with 30,000*l.* a year and diamonds worth a year's income should not be strained. On any occasion, however, on which the commonest knowledge was of real importance, Lady Pargiter was at a great disadvantage ; and such an occasion had now arisen.

When the card of Mr. Brail, Detective Department, Scotland Yard, was handed to her by that gentleman in person (for he it was who had called on her that morning so long before visiting hours), she at once jumped to the conclusion that he had been sent to her by the police. She had heard of Scotland Yard, and she had heard of detectives, and she at once combined her information; if she had known only a little more, if she had even read some of those excellent works of fiction in which the duties of detectives are portrayed, she would have been aware that they are often employed by private individuals. As it was, instead of beholding in the man a possible emissary of Mr. Signet's, she only saw a member of the force which is supported by the ratepayers, and who should naturally be well disposed towards whoever paid the most rates.

'I have called in accordance with instructions,' said Mr. Brail, after a respectful salutation, ' concerning your ladyship's diamonds, which it seems are gone a-missing.'

'My diamonds! and missing! This is the first I have heard of it.' She spoke with great coolness, and apparent deliberation;

but the fact was, that she had answered on the impulse of the moment. It was her rule of life (as having an aristocratic and indifferent air) not to appear moved by any event, so far as outsiders were concerned, and also she thought it good policy to let the policeman tell his own story. It would not only have disgusted but very seriously alarmed her (for she had good cause for alarm) if she had known that what the policeman was saying to himself was, ' That's one lie, my lady, to begin with.'

' Well, ma'am, the fact is, Mr. Helston— he as is Mr. Signet's assistant—is missing, and the jewels of course were in his charge.'

' Of course they were,' assented Lady Pargiter with emphasis.

' Well, ma'am, you see I'm getting up the case, which is a very important one, and I am naturally desirous of obtaining every information.'

' The interests of justice demand it,' said Lady Pargiter approvingly.

' Just so ; it is better for everybody's

sake—except those as have not acted on the square—that I should be supplied with information.'

'There can't be a doubt of it,' said Lady Pargiter; 'nor can there be a doubt,' she added with severity, 'that some person or persons' (this she thought quite a legal touch) 'are not acting, as you call it, on the square.'

'Well, ma'am, yes; there must have been robbery at least.'

'As you say, at least, Mr. Brail—and perhaps something else.'

'I am afraid so, ma'am, indeed. It's even betting as it's murder.'

'I am not of your opinion, Mr. Brail.'

The detective raised his eyes to her rather quicker than was his wont, for all his movements were quiet and methodical.

'It's only my idea,' continued she, with a sense of having said too much. 'Let us hear your story first.'

'Well, ma'am, I've got no story; it isn't my business to have one in these cases, but only to listen to other people's. I've been to Mr. Signet's, of course.'

'Well!' said she impatiently; for he spoke so slowly as almost to appear to have an impediment in his speech.

'He has nothing to say except that Mr. Helston didn't come to his establishment this morning, and consequently did not bring back the jewels. Then, Lady Pargiter, I went to the cabman's; he as brought Mr. Helston to your house. I am bound to say he seems an honest man enough, and to tell a plain tale—though it's a strange one—in a plain way.'

'Very likely: why should he not? Well, what does *he* say?'

'Why, he says—and sticks to it—that he brought Mr. Helston to your house as usual, but never took him away again: that he left him here.'

'Left Mr. Helston in Moor Street? *in my house?*'

('If she's acting,' thought Mr. Brail to himself, 'she's a keen one.') No expression of face or voice could be more instinct with astonishment and even indignation. 'That's what he says, my lady: that Mr. Helston was asked to stop here.'

'Then the man must be mad or drunk. How could such a thing be possible? Do you suppose that my husband—Sir Charles Pargiter—is on visiting terms with a person like this Helston, that he should invite him to remain *here?*' The scorn in her voice was scathing, but it did not scathe Mr. Brail.

'I suppose nothing, my lady,' he answered respectfully; 'my business is only to hear other people's suppositions. Rutherford's— that's the cabman's—supposition is that Mr. Helston was ill with a cold or summut, that the night was a very inclement one, and that therefore he was asked by your lady-ship——'

'By me?' ejaculated Lady Pargiter. 'This is too audacious!'

'Was asked by you—through your foot-man—to remain for a few hours. Here are my notes: yes, "at a quarter past three," said he, " it being very snowy and blusterous, I had just driven off from the door with my fare" (that was Mr. Helston, of course), " when one of the six-footers "—I beg your pardon, my lady, he means footman—" runs after the cab and calls me. I stops and he speaks to Mr. Helston. Mr. Helston tells me to drive back again to the house, and then he goes indoors. In a minute or two the footman comes out again and says that his missus has offered Mr. Helston shelter for the night, and that, being so stormy, he has accepted it. And then I drives away, glad enough to go straight home"— which it seems he did,' concluded Mr. Brail, shutting up his memorandum book.

'It is a falsehood from beginning to end!' exclaimed Lady Pargiter, pale with passion. 'I should as soon have thought of offering such hospitality to the cabman himself.'

'I am to understand from you, then, my lady, that the whole story is a fabrication, am I?' observed Mr. Brail with a sort of gentle importunity. 'For instance, that you never sent your footman after Mr. Helston at all?'

For a moment she hesitated. Then she answered plump enough, 'No, I never did.'

'Very good, ma'am.—Then I have no further observation to offer at present.'

He was about to take up his hat in departure when she stopped him with a movement of her hand, and a curt, 'But *I* have, Mr. Brail.'

'Very good, ma'am; my time is yours;' and he sat down again.

'Since you are here in the interests of justice,' she continued, speaking in a hard, slow tone, 'it is only right you should know the truth—or what I believe to be the truth, Mr. Brail. You said you were desirous to hear the opinions of other people.'

'Quite true, ma'am; any suggestion may be valuable, and especially coming from your ladyship.'

'It is not a suggestion, but a conviction; a conviction forced upon me by the conduct of a certain person of whom this Helston is the mere creature. When I said there was something in this matter worse than robbery, I alluded to what I believe the law terms a conspiracy.'

The detective inclined his head. ' There is such a thing, ma'am, in law, no doubt, and it is a very serious matter.'

' It ought to be a hanging matter,' observed Lady Pargiter with decision. ' Well, if you will take my advice, it is in that direction that you will turn your attention.'

' You think this little affair was undertaken as it were by a company, ma'am ? '

' I do. The man Helston had not the wits for it himself; but a certain opportunity for fraud having presented itself to him, he informed his employer, and the two men concerted the robbery.'

' And would you have any objection, ma'am, to state,' said Mr. Brail, with that grave movement of his head which, without being precisely assent or approval, seemed nevertheless to invite confidence, ' what the opportunity was ? '

'It is a matter that does not affect this inquiry, Mr. Brail; but I have reason to believe there was such an opportunity, and that Mr. Signet took advantage of it.'

'I should suggest there was no necessity for mentioning names, my lady—leastways, at this stage of the business.'

'Very good: of course I speak to you in confidence.'

'Just so, my lady; and there being no witnesses but you and me, it would be difficult to prove a libel; your contention is, I reckon, that, the diamonds having been lost when not in your possession, Mr. Signet is answerable for them.'

'Most certainly it is. Hence arises his miserable device of pretending that his assistant found shelter here last night. That he has suborned the cabman I have no sort of doubt.'

'Then where is it—if I may make so bold—that in your ladyship's opinion Mr. Helston is?'

'I believe he is in hiding somewhere

yet not so closely hid but that Mr. Signet can find him. A man like that can take my diamonds and set them afresh so that none of them can be recognised. It is a cheaper way even than giving me half their value for them, as he once had the hardihood to offer;' and Lady Pargiter's face, which had been pale enough during some portions of the interview, flushed with the remembrance of that outrage.

'Well, my lady, I will take to heart what you say,' said Mr. Brail, ' and by putting two and two together make no doubt that I shall come to the bottom of this matter. Good morning, and many thanks to your ladyship.'

The instant he had parted from her, Lady Pargiter rang for her maid.

' You did what I told you with respect to Harvey?' said she quickly; ' I mean, as to telling him to hold his tongue?'

'Certainly I did, my lady.'

'And you said it as from yourself, and not from me?'

'Well, of course, my lady,' replied Patty, with a smile that seemed to say, 'Am I an idiot?' 'I laid every injunction upon Harvey directly I left your ladyship's presence, and, to do him justice, he was willing enough to oblige me, only——'

'Only what?' inquired her mistress impatiently.

'Well, I am afraid it was a little late, my lady, for the first man as this Mr. Brail came across—indeed, he opened the door to him—was Harvey: and the first question he put to him was, "Did your mistress happen to send you after Mr. Helston's cab last night?" When, meaning no harm, he told the truth, and said, "Yes, she did."'

Lady Pargiter made no reply; only lisped out the word 'dolt,' and sank into a chair; but if those who averred that her ladyship's face was 'incapable of expression' could have seen it at that moment, they would have confessed their error.

CHAPTER XXVI.

PUBLICITY.

IT was characteristic of the quiet little household in Cavendish Grove that it took in no daily newspaper : Uncle Stephen was wont to aver that sooner or later he was sure to hear any news that was worth hearing, while all that was worthless died away and never reached him ; while Matthew was too wrapped up in his own thoughts, and in the causes of Madge's failure, to interest himself in the affairs of the day. But of late ' the flying buttress,' as Mr. Frank Barlow had been named by Sabey, because of his propinquity, and also from his intimate relations with the family, kept the ladies at least *au courant* with all that was going on. He was ' of the day, daily,' as Uncle Stephen said, both by nature and calling, and the morning newspaper, and indeed the evening, was as the breath of life to him. On the morning after Matthew's disappearance, however, he found his favourite journal a little *too* interesting; like a man who, though accustomed to quinine, takes six grains instead of two, and discovers that a tonic has its drawbacks. The shock, nevertheless, although severe, was far from unexpected ; he had been well aware that that little paragraph in the *Night Cap* would grow like a mushroom (or rather, like rankest toadstool) and be served in the morning, in its new shape, at every breakfast-table in the kingdom. The 'Mysterious disappearance of a jeweller's assistant,' was now transformed into ' Great Jewel Robbery,' and the circumstance of Matthew being missing was made subordinate to the loss of ' those diamonds which on the person of their owner, Lady Pargiter, have been so long a familiar object with all frequenters of the haunts of Fashion.' It was wonderful, considering the short time that had elapsed since the occurrence, how accurate, on the whole, were the details; but at the same time, as it seemed to Mr. Barlow, the paragraph had the appearance of being more or less 'inspired;' it took for granted the loss of the jewels would fall upon 'the respectable and long-established firm of Star and Signet,' whom it condoled with accordingly; but it especially condoled with Lady Pargiter, whom 'no mere sum of money could recompense for a *parure* which was practically priceless, as well as endeared to her by hereditary association.' The sting of the narrative, however—which was a pretty long one—lay in its tail: for it concluded with these words, 'We understand that the missing personage, Matthew Helston, had been entrusted with the custody of the jewels only on one or two previous occasions, and had been in the service of Messrs. Star and Signet but a few months.'

'These people are worth powder and shot, that's some comfort,' was Mr. Barlow's first exclamation on reading this unpleasant remark; 'let them only speak out a trifle more plainly, and, by Jove, they shall pay for it. But, in the mean time, what a blow it will be for Amy and her sister! They're sure to see it, however, or something worse; and at all events some "damned good-natured friend" is sooner or later certain to tell them all about it. I'd better take it in and get it over.'

Accordingly he took it in and showed it to Uncle Stephen and Amy; the former agreed with him that it was only what was to have been expected, but the latter was vehemently indignant. She only wished the man who wrote such words of Matthew could but have seen his wife, as she had seen her, sleepless, desolate, despairing.

'My dear Amy,' said Uncle Stephen, 'he would only have made another paragraph about *her*—and cleared, perhaps, seven-and-sixpence by it. Do you really mean that Sabey has had no sleep?'

'I believe, none; I have stolen into her room at all hours, and found her watching; sitting, lying, or standing, it is all the same with her; her eyes are never closed, and begin to have a haunted look in them which terrifies me. The very child at times seems frightened at her, and cries distressingly. Should she see this paper I should tremble for her reason.'

'Yet it had no ill effect on *you*, who are her other self,' observed Uncle Stephen; 'I noticed that, on the contrary, it made you pluck up spirit.'

'To let Mrs. Helston see it would be a dangerous experiment,' remarked Mr. Barlow, 'in her present weak condition.'

'There is nothing so bad as suspense, in my opinion,' argued the old man. 'Any change from that would be a change for the better. If you could persuade her that her husband's honour is impugned, and needs defending, that would put heart into her.'

'She needs it,' murmured Amy, with a deep sigh.

At this moment there was a violent ring at the front door.

'Did I not hear a bell?' said Uncle

Stephen, as though a 34-pounder had been fired at one's ear, and one had asked, ' Did not something go off just now ? '

Amy rushed into the hall, to find Mr. Signet stamping flakes of snow there off his boots, which he had incurred in his passage from the cab, and inquiring of the servant for herself.

' My dear Miss Thurlow, you are the very person I came to see,' said he effusively.

' Is there any news, Mr. Signet ? '

' Well, scarcely news : but I promised to come, you know, if anything occurred.'

' It is very kind of you, I'm sure. Oh, Mr. Signet, do you bring us hope ? '

' Well, at all events this will help us,' he said, holding up the same newspaper which Mr. Barlow had just brought. ' Publicity is always useful in these cases ; but of all the disgraceful, abominable statements——'

' Is that you, Mr. Signet ? ' exclaimed a broken voice at the top of the stairs.

' Yes, ma'am, it's me,' returned the jeweller, not very graciously. ' I hope I

find you as well as can be expected. I will
come to you, if you wish it, in one minute,
but I want to say two words in private to
Miss Thurlow.'

'Oh, Frank, here is Mr. Signet,' said
Amy, as Mr. Barlow made his appearance in
the hall with a frown on his usually pleasant
face. 'He has something to say' (here she
dropped her voice) 'that he does not wish
dear Sabey to hear.'

'You will keep nothing from me, Amy,'
pleaded Sabey from the floor above, as
though she had heard her words. 'Oh, let
me hear what Mr. Signet has to say.'

Her voice was so pitiful, mingled as it
was with the querulous cry of the child, that
it went to Amy's heart.

'I must go to my sister,' she said hur-
riedly; 'pray Mr. Signet, say all you wish
to Mr. Barlow, and to Uncle Stephen. They
will know what it is best for her to hear.'

Since it seemed that all chance of a *tête-
à-tête* was over for the present, the jeweller
followed Mr. Barlow into the parlour.

'This is a sad business,' said Mr. Durham, as he held out his hand to the visitor.

'Ah, you have seen the paper; sad is no word for it. It is disgusting that the press should lend itself to such manœuvres.'

'Manœuvres!' echoed Uncle Stephen. 'It seems to me that is a mild term for the implication conveyed.'

'You are right, Mr. Durham; it is an *ex parte* statement of the vilest kind.'

'Why *does* he talk about an *ex parte* statement?' mused Uncle Stephen, looking at Mr. Signet with much curiosity; 'why is it, I wonder, that all these good people use foreign tongues so much? They are like bad cooks, that serve up everything, even though it is very good of itself, with walnut ketchup.'

'It is obvious to me,' continued Mr. Signet, 'that the man who wrote this notice has been got at by Lady Pargiter. It must have cost her ten pounds at least—and I hope twenty. The idea of "no sum of money" recompensing that woman for her diamonds, when to my knowledge she has done her best to get rid of them for the last three months! And then his alluding to my responsibility as being an acknowledged fact, when it is by no means certain she has not got them all the time in Moor Street! I call it disgusting and disgraceful.'

'I had an idea that you might be alluding to the rather unpleasant charge this paper makes by implication against my nephew,' observed Mr. Durham drily.

'Well, and that's bad too, sir—very bad,' admitted Mr. Signet.

'But still, the loss of one's character is nothing as compared with the loss of one's money,' added Uncle Stephen, with a philosophic air.

'Well, it must be a deuced good character if it's worth 25,000*l*.,' rejoined Mr. Signet. 'I don't know one that would fetch that money myself.'

'Are we to understand that you have nothing further to communicate to us,' inquired Mr. Barlow stiffly, 'beyond what we had already learnt for ourselves from the newspaper?'

'I did not come to communicate even *that* to *you*, sir,' replied Mr. Signet tartly. 'I have a request to make to Miss Thurlow. She was under the expectation that when the time was ripe I should do so. Indeed, we made an arrangement together to that effect.'

'You are perhaps unaware, Mr. Signet,' returned Mr. Barlow, 'that it is not usual for gentlemen who are in no way connected with them to make private arrangements with young ladies. If you have anything to say to Miss Thurlow, you will be good enough to do so through me, who have the honour to be her destined husband.'

'You are a business man, I understand, Mr. Barlow,' returned Mr. Signet coldly, 'and if so, you should know that business matters—when of a confidential kind—as this happens to be—are conducted between principals without the interference of a third party. You have no *locus standi* in the matter whatever.'

'There he is again!' muttered Uncle Stephen. 'I am curious to see, when Barlow pulls his nose (which will happen presently), whether he will even *then* speak plain English.'

'You are talking of what you don't understand, Mr. Signet, and also very impertinently,' said Mr. Barlow. 'You shall not see Miss Thurlow alone, either now or at any other time, I promise you. If you go upstairs at all, it will be in my company.'

'Then I shall go upstairs to no purpose, since I do not choose to speak what I have to say in your hearing,' returned Mr. Signet.

Here Amy appeared at the door, like some sweet divinity of old, to appease the wrath of warring mortals.

'If you wouldn't mind coming to see my sister, Mr. Signet, she would take it very kind of you. She is growing impatient to hear your news. I think, Frank,' added she, as Mr. Barlow rose with the obvious intention of forming one of the party, 'that

too many of us at a time oppress poor
Sabey; it will be better if she and I were to
see Mr. Signet alone.'

'It seems to me natural enough,' observed Uncle Stephen, as Mr. Barlow stood
irresolute; he was ashamed, under circumstances so sad, and in the presence of innocent unconscious Amy, to show his jealousy
—nor, indeed, was he jealous of her at all;
but he was very loath to give up his point.
Poor Matthew's dislike of Mr. Signet had
been as a pin's point to a barbed arrow's in
comparison with the prejudice he himself
now entertained against that gentleman.'

'Would not Sabey prefer to see this—to
see Mr. Signet alone?' he said: a propo-
sition manifestly weak even to the suggester
of it.

I once knew an eminent yet perfectly
honest country solicitor, who was accused,
as a last resource, or rather as a parting
stroke of malevolence, by a scoundrel against
whom he had been professionally engaged, of
forgery. If this thing had happened to a

client, he would have laughed it to scorn;
but since he himself was concerned, it quite
threw him off his mental balance, and he
telegraphed to London for the first legal
advice procurable, as though a man stung
by a nettle should have sent post-haste to
the Queen's surgeon. And so it was with
prudent, sensible Mr. Barlow; now that his
own toes were trodden upon, he lost all his
judicial calm, and showed himself as sensi-
tive—and, to say truth, as unreasonable—as
though he had been a poet instead of an
attorney.

'Will Sabey see Mr. Signet alone?'
repeated wondering Amy. 'Why, no,
Frank. I think it very advisable that I
should be with her. You can scarcely
understand the sad state which she is in.
Please step this way, Mr. Signet;' which
Mr. Signet did with no little nimbleness and
triumph.

He felt that he had scored considerably
off Mr. Frank Barlow, who had moreover
given him some useful hints as to his

behaviour ; for, to confess the honest truth, the imputation which the newspaper had made against Matthew Helston had not made much impression on the jeweller. He had come to Cavendish Grove so full of his own grievances and his affection for Amy, that there had not been much room for sympathy upon his assistant's account. But he now understood that under that roof at least the anxiety on this head was very considerable.

Moreover, he could not help observing that the effect it had wrought upon Matthew Helston's wife was great and deplorable. That look of extreme youth which had once been her peculiarity had fled, though not, alas ! what had been an accompaniment of it, her appearance of fragility.

It begot the same sort of tender sadness in the beholder that is awakened by the skeleton of a flower, or the dying echo of a song. You said to yourself involuntarily as your eye fell on her, 'She is not long for this world,' and, indeed, even now she

hardly seemed to belong to the world at all.
It is not, unhappily, a rare case among the
lower classes, though seldom among the
middle or the very low. You come too often
across these sad transparencies; women
whom Fate would seem to have formed to
bear light burdens, but on whom the heaviest
—poverty, shame, neglect, anxieties, trouble
of all sorts—have been imposed; beings
whose delicate frame has been worn away
as it were by attrition of the rough world,
and through which the very soul shines,
about to flee.

She held a thin hand out to the jeweller,
who took it respectfully, and with a sudden
impulse raised it to his lips. ' I am deeply
grieved, madam,' he said, with a genuine
though passing reverence for her great
sorrow, ' for the calamity that has befallen
you.'

' And you, sir, also have suffered,' she
said gently, ' though '—and here she sighed
in spite of herself—' though in another way.'

' Don't speak of it,' said Mr. Signet. ' I

am menaced, no doubt, with a serious loss, but at the worst it is not irreparable.'

'True,' she murmured, 'true: whereas, with the exception of my dear sister and—and—our little one, I have lost my all.'

'Tut, tut, my dear madam,' said Mr. Signet encouragingly: 'all is not lost that seems so. Your husband must be *somewhere*, you know, and we must find him. That's the point; we must find him, and the jewels too. I had some talk with your good sister here—perhaps she told you of it.'

'She told me that you had been very good and kind about this matter, Mr. Signet.'

'Not at all, my dear madam, not at all; only common feeling, I assure you; except, of course, that I feel an interest—I may say, a strong personal interest—in whatever concerns her—and you—and of course in Mr. Helston himself. That is what I am come about to-day. The accusation directed against him in the newspaper this morning——'

Hitherto, save for the first moment of

the jeweller's entrance, Mrs. Helston had leant back in her chair, with her eyes resting upon him, but with scarcely more speculation in them than in those of a corpse; they seemed to look right through him, and fix themselves on vacancy beyond; his words had reached the doorway of her mind—for she had understood their import—but had passed away from it without crossing its threshold. But ere he finished his last sentence, the colour had rushed to her wan cheeks, and she was sitting upright in her chair like one whom a miracle has restored to life. 'Accusation? What accusation?' she inquired with a fierce astonishment.

'Well, perhaps I should not say accusation, Mrs. Helston,' said Mr. Signet smoothly. 'I think innuendo would be the better word.'

'Do you mean that some one has dared to hint anything ill of Matthew—of my husband?'

'Well, it's only a paragraph in a newspaper, after all,' observed Mr. Signet, not a little alarmed by the effect of his own exordium. 'When incidents of this mysterious kind occur, it is but too usual——'

'Let me see the paper—I pray you let me see it, Mr. Signet,' she added pleadingly, ' with my own eyes.'

He pulled it out of his pocket, not without compunction—though he had come to the house with that express purpose—and, placing it in her hand, pointed out the offending lines with his stumpy finger. 'What it states is that I am responsible for the jewels, since they were lost while in my agent's custody, and what it suggests is that my agent has absconded with them.'

' Absconded ! Matthew absconded !' exclaimed Sabey, her eyes flashing like the very gems of which he spoke, and her clenched fingers tightening as though she would have struck the slanderer down. 'Who dares to say so?'

' It is no matter who, my dear madam ; ten thousand people, having read this paragraph, will have already said so, and to-morrow there will be a million. It is out of the million that the juries come. That is the object of this infernal woman—to influence the jury.'

'What woman?' inquired Sabey. She was all attention now; not a word escaped her, or lost a shred of its meaning.

'Lady Pargiter.'

'A bad woman,' murmured Sabey, with her distant look again; 'a woman without a heart.'

'Very true, madam; but unhappily not without a head. She is as deep as a well, though with no truth at the bottom of her. I came here to let you know who are Mr. Helston's friends and who are his enemies. This woman is an enemy. I have reason to believe—nay, I know—that she has stated it to be her conviction that your husband and myself have conspired to steal her diamonds. The gentlemen below stairs seemed to think I cared for the jewels only; I will only say they have misconceived my feelings—and my motives.'

'Which I think—nay, I believe—do you honour,' said Amy warmly. She did really believe that Mr. Signet had been unjustly treated by Frank, and she resented it.

'I thank you, Miss Thurlow,' replied the jeweller. 'What I would wish to feel is that Mr. Helston and I are in one boat in this affair. That he is as blameless as myself I have no doubt. But we must all of us pull together. I will keep you informed of every step I take, and I must beg of you to do the like. There must be no divided councils.'

'My sister and I are in your hands,' said Amy simply. 'We have confidence both in your good will and your ability to help us.'

She glanced at Sabey for some corroboration of this view. 'I believe in a just God,' she answered gravely, 'who will not suffer Matthew's memory to be wronged and slandered.'

'Quite right,' assented Mr. Signet approvingly, 'and I hope those who do it will be punished; Lady Pargiter for one. We are going to work at first, of necessity, in the dark, but I think I see daylight somewhere even now. Only, you and I—and Mrs. Helston, here—we must pull together.'

Miss Thurlow inclined her head, and began to hope the interview was over: for she had been much more discomposed by it—on more than one account—than she had appeared to be. But Mr. Signet had something else to say, though he said it in a very low and confidential tone. 'Have you spoken to your sister about that matter of the portrait, Miss Thurlow?'

'No, indeed,' said she, with almost a frightened air; for the miniature of Matthew, to which she had referred with comparative indifference when questioned by the jeweller, was now scarcely ever out of Sabey's hands, and, when it was so, lay in her bosom. 'I hope that will not be insisted on.'

'It will be very desirable to have it,' said Mr. Signet doubtfully.

'What is wanted?' inquired Sabey, understanding the drift though not the exact subject of this talk. 'I hope that no inconvenience, or distress, or pain of any kind that may be caused me will be suffered to interfere with doing the best that can be done.'

'My dear madam,' said Mr. Signet, 'permit me to congratulate you upon your admirable common sense. In circumstances of this kind it is sometimes necessary to sacrifice one's feelings. As to convenience, publicity, as we have just had occasion to observe, is highly inconvenient and—and— even offensive; but then its utility is beyond question. Now, supposing your excellent husband should have been carried away by wicked persons, or if any serious accident (which Heaven forbid) should have incapacitated him from communicating with his friends, or even making known his own identity, what a thing it would be if his features were made familiar to the public! The photographic art can multiply likenesses indefinitely. The Government itself makes use of it in—in various establishments. The dead, the drowned, before interment——'

'You had better tell my sister what you wish at once, Mr. Signet,' interrupted Amy; 'if, indeed, she has not already guessed it.'

'Oh, Amy, must I give up his picture?' pleaded Sabey, drawing the miniature from her bosom, and gazing on it with passionate fondness. 'He gave it me with his own hands on his last birthday—the last.' And, with one heart-wrung sob at the thought that he would have no birthday more, she pressed it to her lips, and covered her face with her hands.

'Let us congratulate ourselves, my dear madam, that it was the last,' observed Mr. Signet consolingly, 'since, the more recent the date, the more accurate will probably be the likeness. It pains me to ask for a memento so dear to you, but the article will be returned, of course, without chip or flaw.' Here he found himself slipping into a trade formula, and floundered out of it as well as he could. 'In fact, it will not be a penny the worse for being photographed.'

'I know you will not let them be longer

about it than is absolutely necessary,' said Amy, taking the miniature from her sister's unresisting hand, and beckoning Mr. Signet from the room. 'As to its safe custody, I need not tell you that, with the fate of its original in this terrible doubt, this picture is priceless.'

'I will guard it, my dear Miss Thurlow,' returned the jeweller, placing it in his breast-pocket, 'more jealously for your sake than if it were set with rubies.'

The assurance, perhaps, smacked a little of the shop, but the air and manner with which it was conveyed quite recalled the age of chivalry.

To Mr. Barlow, standing in the hall and looking upward, with the fixed resolution of not giving Mr. Signet an opportunity of seeing Amy alone when they should leave her sister's presence, they recalled a good many things :—How this fellow had had the impudence to present his 'intended' with a ring ; how he had got up a water-party on her account ; how he had 'soft-sawdered' her—such, I regret to say, was the expression which suggested itself to Mr. Barlow—as respected his interest in Matthew; and, finally, how he had contrived to establish himself on such terms with her that he could lay his hand upon his heart—for he had put the picture in his left breast-pocket—while wishing her good-bye. He felt he could not trust himself to speak with Mr. Signet without speaking his mind; he therefore measured him from top to toe, as if he had been his tailor with an order for an outfit, and watched him pass out without a word.

If he could have looked into Mr. Signet's heart of hearts he would not, perhaps, have been so discomposed; for though on pleasure he had been bent (so far as Amy was concerned), the jeweller had had a frugal mind; he had, in fact, come to Cavendish Grove on business, though it had gratified him to transact it with the object of his affections; he had felt that it was of importance to him that the family and himself should act together in the matter of Helston's disappearance; that it should be known to the world at large that he had every confidence in his late assistant's integrity, and was on terms of intimacy with his friends. That the newspaper writer should have condoled with him was bad; but far the worst part of the paragraph in his eyes was that which took Helston's complicity in the loss of the diamonds for granted, for the *facit per alium facit per se* of the law was fatally applicable to him. On the other hand, his motive in getting possession of the portrait was entirely different. Mr. Brail, as we have seen, had frankly revealed to him the imputations so imprudently made against him by Lady Pargiter; nor had he concealed from him certain suspicious circumstances in that inter-view—including one downright falsehood—which had told against that lady herself; but, nevertheless, the impression on the detective's mind was on the whole what it had been from the first—namely, that Matthew Helston had absconded with the jewels.

'It's a police case, Mr. Signet, and nothing else, that's certain,' he had said; 'and what is almost as certain, to my thinking, is that your man has walked off with the swag. If you can get his picture, it is only a question of sooner or later as to getting *him*. But time is priceless in these cases. It should be in every police station in London within twelve hours.'

This is what Mr. Signet had euphemistically termed ' the advantage of publicity.'

CHAPTER XXVII.

A SUPERFLUOUS PRECAUTION.

APART from the portrait of his missing assistant, and the furtherance (as he imagined) of his suit with Amy, it was not very much that Mr. Signet had obtained from his visit to Cavendish Grove; but it was something. It was important to him, as we have said, to show that he for his part entertained the highest confidence in Matthew Helston and continued to do so; that he and Matthew's belongings were as good friends as ever, notwithstanding what had occurred; and it still more behoved him to strengthen and to keep steadfast all testimony that told for Matthew. At present this was confined to that of John Rutherford the cabman; not a very weighty witness, it may be thought, against the direct evidence of Lady Pargiter and her

servants, but still (as Mr. Brail had reported)
'dependable.' Moreover, supposing he had
not been bribed by Matthew—an idea that
was rigidly excluded from Mr. Signet's present calculations—what motive could he have
had for falsehood? Mr. Signet had been
told by Mr. Brail that 'if he meant to make
a fight for it'—that is, to decline to pay
Lady Pargiter for the loss of the diamonds—
he had better not visit Hybla Mews in
person.

'They will say,' urged the detective,
'that you got at the man, and paid him to
stick to his story—which is already, I must
confess, to my thinking very much in the
cock-and-bull line.'

But inclined as the jeweller was to follow
the police agent's advice in the main, and to
attach much weight to his opinions (when
they did not tend to despair of his own
chances), he found this prohibition too hard
to be obeyed. Like a child who has a dor-
mouse he is forbidden to stroke, Mr. Signet
hankered after his only witness, and could

not understand how he could be damaged by a little handling. He had not the least intention of cramming him for cross-examination, or of suggesting to him any fact that might not have come to his own knowledge; but he wanted to see what manner of man he was, and to hear with his own ears the details of that strange story on the maintenance or breaking down of which so much depended. The largeness of his stake in the matter was of course the main reason of his acceptance of the cabman's theory; but his dislike of Lady Pargiter—which by this time, indeed, had grown to positive hatred—undoubtedly made it more grateful to him.

On leaving Cavendish Grove his usual course would have been citywards; but he bade his driver put him down at Hybla Terrace, at the corner of which he dismissed him. He did not wish the man to know that he was about to visit the Mews.

As he neared the 'Rising Sun' he came upon an unkempt shambling creature, certainly attached to the public-house in one sense, and probably so in another, of whom he inquired John Rutherford's number; but the man professed ignorance, and referred him to the inn.

Under any other circumstances—even in his improved ones of late days—Mr. Richard Dartmoor would certainly have been met with slouching under the portico, or speculating with his hands in his pockets upon the solid content of the edifice from without; but he had disappeared within the last ten hours, almost as suddenly as poor Matthew Helston. The cause of this was remarkable. Mr. Dartmoor had been slouching and speculating as usual on the preceding afternoon, when, on emerging from the inn after a refreshing 'dram,' he had suddenly come upon the very person whom Mr. Signet had just met. This dissolute lounger and loafer was so exceedingly like himself that the effect was almost the same upon him as that of the Doppel-gänger upon a German, or that species of second sight called 'the double'

upon a Scotchman. Imagine a person of
nervous temperament (much aggravated by
liquor), who, intending a practical joke,
dresses himself up as a spectre; and instead
of his victim meets in a lonely place a real
ghost—and you will have some sort of idea
of the state of mind into which Mr. Richard
Dartmoor was thrown by this *rencontre.*

He toddled back to the inn for a tonic
dram, and then slouched out by the swing-
door on the other side, not certain of his
future movements, *i.e.* whether he would
not shift his quarters, and leave the 'Rising
Sun' for good and all, rather than face such.
visions; when what should he see within a
few yards of him but another counterfeit
presentment of himself. '*Voilà deux*—there
are two!' he would have exclaimed, like
the Black Mousquetaire of Thomas Ingoldsby,
had he been familiar with the quotation; as
it was, he murmured—'Blue-bottles, by
gum!' Then he looked up to the sky with
a careless air, as though snowflakes were
thistledown, and south-easters zephyrs; and

not gradually, like the youth who 'journeys
farther from the East,' but at a much more
rapid rate, increased his distance from the
' Rising Sun.'

Unconscious of the loss which Society in
the neighbourhood of Hybla Terrace had
thus received, Mr. Signet entered the Mews,
and was directed to Mr. Rutherford's dwelling.   He had a certain right to intrude upon
the cabman's privacy, inasmuch as the latter
was well aware that he had defrayed—
through Matthew Helston—the very considerable sums that had gone into 'honest
John's' pocket in payment of those nightly
expeditions to Moor Street, the last of which
had ended so disastrously.

The door was opened to him by Sally,
who always performed that office.

' I am Mr. Signet,' he said frankly ; ' you
will know what I am come about.'

' I know very well,' she said. ' You have
sent the police after my poor husband, but
he is not a bit frightened.   He is as honest
a man as you are, and he has told no lies.'

'I hope not,' said Mr. Signet, in a very genuine manner. ' "Tell the truth and stick to it" should be every Englishman's motto. If you will allow me, I will walk upstairs.'

Perhaps he had read in ' Hints on Etiquette ' that in getting over stiles and going upstairs one should precede a lady, or perhaps he wished to see Mr. Rutherford before his wife should announce his presence; but at all events Mr. Signet did precede her.

He found the cabman still in his sleeved waistcoat, as Mr. Brail had found him. He had been too much disturbed in his mind to complete his toilette, far less to take out his cab as usual, and he was smoking his sixteenth pipe.

' Oh, here's another, is there ? ' he growled.

' It's Mr. Signet, John,' put in Sally hastily.

' What do I care who it is ? '

' Of course you don't,' said the jeweller ; ' an honest man should have no apprehensions.'

'Apprehensions be hanged!' exclaimed Mr. Rutherford. 'Of course I shall be apprehended. Poor folks always are when rich folks have mislaid things or made away with them. I knew a man as was transported for life for stealing a watch that was all the time in an old lady's watch-pocket over her bed, and who was so fortunate after a year or two as to get the Queen's pardon for it; but it isn't everybody as has his good luck.'

'That was a sad mistake indeed,' said the jeweller sympathisingly. 'But it cannot have occurred in this case. Would you be so good as to tell me what you know about this Moor Street business—the same story, I mean, that you told the person who called on you this morning? Have you got such a thing as pen and ink, Mrs. Rutherford?'

A bright thought here struck the jeweller. He would set the man's narrative down in writing, and get him to sign it. If it was of no other use, it would be always handy to refresh Mr. Rutherford's memory.

Sally produced a washing-book, the stump of a pen, and an ink-bottle—the contents of which were so dried up that it had to be liquefied like the blood of St. Januarius. Mr. Signet, however, was deft with his fingers, and could write with anything. John narrated the story with which we are acquainted, more doggedly than before, but almost in the same words. 'If you was to squeeze me between the keb doors of my own 'ansom,' he said, 'you would always have the same story.'

Mr. Signet looked at him as though he had been an Early Martyr prepared to suffer for the faith—and perhaps even with a greater admiration.

'Now be so kind, my excellent fellow, as to set your name to this, which I have written down from your own lips.'

'No, I couldn't do that,' said honest John; 'I really couldn't.'

'Not sign it? Then do you mean to say it's not true, you scoundrel?'

Mr. Signet would probably have proceeded to use much stronger language had not Mrs. Rutherford whispered something in his ear.

'Oh, can't write, can't he? He can make his mark, I suppose?'

'If you call me a scoundrel again I'll make a pretty big mark between your eyes,' exclaimed John irascibly.

'He's honesty itself,' murmured Mr. Signet, in a rapture at this menace. 'He'd be worth his weight in—well, in seed pearls—before the Lord Chief Justice. Stop one moment—we must have a witness, and it mustn't be his wife.' Mr. Signet stepped to the 'verander,' and put his head out. Immediately opposite, smoking a straw and speculating after the manner of his kind, was the man to whom he had applied in vain for Mr. Rutherford's address.

'Hi, come here!' he cried authoritatively. The man slouched carelessly across the yard, though the wind was keen enough to have quickened the steps of a sloth.

'Can you write?' inquired the jeweller.

'Ay,' replied the other, so gloomily that one might have thought the knowledge of that art—upon the principle of a little learning being a dangerous thing—had brought him into his present unprosperous condition.

'Then come up here.'

Not without some pride in the device which his own legal acumen had suggested, Mr. Signet pointed out the spot in the washing-book where the cabman was to put his cross, and the witness to subscribe his name. The materials he had to work with were crude enough, but every formality was complied with. Mr. Rutherford evinced a decided gratification in repeating the words, 'Witness my act and deed' after the jeweller; and when the latter murmured, with a sigh of satisfaction, *Litera scripta manet,* honest John nodded approvingly, as though that mystic sentence had been the one thing necessary to accomplish the rite.

'Money,' said Mr. Signet, addressing the stranger, who stood with his eyes glancing furtively about him and with his hand passing slowly over his mouth, as though in fond imagination removing the traces of liquor, 'I am unable to give you for this service; but I dare say a dram of something short would be acceptable this cold morning. Mrs. Rutherford, can you oblige me so far?'

Sally at once produced a bottle of gin, and Mr. John Jones, messenger, of Rose Court, Oxford Street—for such, it appeared from his signature, was his style and title— having accepted her hospitality, ducked his shock of hair and shambled out.

'What I have said to yonder fellow, I must say to you, John,' continued the jeweller: 'what you have done this morning must go without any immediate fee or reward. No man, says the law, must be paid for telling the truth.'

'I quite understand that, sir,' answered Mr. Rutherford naïvely, 'for then everybody would tell the truth, and where would the lawyers be?'

'But henceforth remember, Star and Signet are your friends, my man. They will see you through this business, and when that's done will show their gratitude.'

'What I should like better than money —though money's allus acceptable to a poor man, Mr. Signet—is to see that 'ere Lady Pargiter trounced. It's her as has been the cause of all this from first to last; and it's her as has got Master Matthew and them diamonds—I'll lay my life on it.'

'Give me your hand, John,' said Mr. Signet effusively;—'I wish I could put something in it, but I dare not. An honest man's the noblest work of Providence.—Lest your memory should ever want refreshing, by-the by, concerning this matter, I'll have a copy made of this little document, and your wife will read it out to you—you *can* read, my good woman, can't you?'

'Read!' exclaimed John with indignation. 'Just you wait and hear her! Sally, give him that account of the Tetbury Pet's performance in last week's *Hera*.'

'Not just now; another day,' said Mr. Signet hastily. 'God bless you both! We shall always know where to find you when you're wanted, shan't we, John? Good-bye!'

'Wanted!' growled Mr. Rutherford, as the jeweller tripped downstairs. 'Oh, that's what it comes to after all, is it? You're hand and glove with the *Perleece*, are yer?'

Ignorant of the offence he had thus given, Mr. Signet hurried to Paulet Street, where he found Mr. Brail awaiting him.

'You have news?' said that gentleman, perceiving a look of triumph in his employer's face.

'Not exactly news, but I think I have done a good stroke of work this morning. I've got Rutherford's evidence in black and white, and here it is.'

'And in your handwriting too,' observed Mr. Brail drily. 'That will be of interest to your friends, no doubt, sir; but it will not increase the value of the document in the eyes of a jury.'

'Well, the man couldn't write, you see,' said Mr. Signet, a good deal taken aback by this remark; 'and then, I took care to get a witness.'

'So I see; John Jones, messenger, Rose Court, Oxford Street—um! Well, I don't know the gentleman by name, but I seem to know his handwriting. Where did you pick him up?'

'In Hybla Mews; a perfect stranger, and therefore an independent witness, I conclude.'

'Not so very independent, Mr. Signet. He's one of the two watchers as I set myself to look after the cabman.'

'Bless my soul!' said Mr. Signet.

'Well, I did tell you, leave everything in my hands, sir,' continued Mr. Brail severely; 'when you employ a Detective, it's better to do that than to meddle with a matter yourself. Amateurs is more harm than good, you may rely on't.—Now listen to me, for I've got a *fact* for you—a fact worth twenty washingbooks full of noughts and crosses. A young woman has just been here with a *communication.*'

'A young woman! You mean Miss Thurlow, I suppose!'

'No, I don't; she was quite another sort of young woman—one as knows what's what, I guess, and the price of it. I only caught a glimpse of her through the shop-door, just now, but I'd seen her once before to-day— as I passed through the hall in Moor Street. She was muffled up, and wore a thick veil, when she asked your shopman if Mr. Signet was in; but I don't forget faces in a hurry. So I just stepped out—as a friend of the firm —to ask her business. She's Lady Pargiter's maid.'

'And what *was* her business?'

'You're to hear that to-morrow. But I found out this much, that she hates her mistress like the devil, and has got a grudge against her, with the means of paying her out. She gave me to understand she only dealt with principals—which means a lot of money.'

'What does that matter?' exclaimed Mr. Signet impatiently. 'Do you think she knows anything?'

' Ay, I do. I'm inclined to think you're right after all. It's Lady Pargiter as is at the bottom of this business, and her maid knows it.'

' I said so! I was sure of it!' exclaimed Mr. Signet excitedly. ' But why did you let her go away?'

Because she said she had no time to spare, and her absence would excite suspicion. To-morrow's her Sunday out. She's got the key of the whole mystery, and—you mark my words—she will come here to sell it.'

CHAPTER XXVIII.

A TRAITRESS IN THE CAMP.

WE know that Mr. Signet was, in intention at least, even at his comparatively advanced period of life, a man of gallantry, but it is probable that even in the hey-day of his youthful prime he had never looked forward with such excitement to the arrival of a fair visitor as he did on that Sunday morning to the coming of Miss Patty Selwood. It was not the evanescent passion for a pretty face, for he had never seen the young woman; whether she was short or tall, dark or fair, was no matter to him whatever. Mr. Brail had told him she was young, and he preferred her so to be, as it was probable he might make a better bargain with her; but otherwise, for all he cared, she might have been of the age in which Sir Cornewall Lewis refused to believe—a hundred—provided she retained her memory. That was the one thing important to him. She was coming, he felt, to tell him what she knew about Lady Pargiter and her diamonds.

She was to leave Moor Street at half-past ten, partly because by that time she would have made her ladyship presentable to the public, and partly because it was the hour for Public Worship, and by a polite fiction, common to establishments of all degrees, the waiting-maid was supposed to be going to church. Not, of course, that 'my lady's maid' was to be seen on a Sunday morning with a prayer-book folded inside her pocket-handkerchief like any Mary Anne or Eliza Jane in ordinary domestic service. If she did have a prayer-book (which is doubtful), it was carried without ostentation ; and so neat and well chosen was her apparel, that unless you had seen her come out of the area gate of No. 10, you would never have believed her to be a servant at all. That is to say, a man would not have done so ; but I believe (such is the marvellous discernment of the sex in such matters) that his wife would have detected it at a glance. *She* would have known that the silk dress was a cheap silk, and the pretty collar of lace only a few pence a yard. It was not Miss Selwood's custom, indeed, to wear either cheap silks or inferior collars on her 'Sundays out,' for on such occasions she was wont to lay Lady Pargiter's wardrobe under contribution ; but on this particular day she wore her own clothes. The reason of this was that she had a fixed intention of breaking with her mistress, and to a delicate mind there were therefore obvious reasons why she should cease to put herself under obligations to her ; it may also be added that, having determined to dig up the hatchet, she was exceedingly cautious not to give her ladyship an opportunity of doing her an ill turn. It was indeed in the highest degree unlikely that Lady Pargiter would miss any particular garments out of her very extensive collection, or even recognise them on Miss Selwood's back ; but that young lady was so prudent that, rather than run the risk, she had sacrificed even her personal vanity.

In a ball-dress, with the Pargiter diamonds on her, Miss Selwood would have made a great sensation; and even without them, and as she was, in her modest 'wraps'—for the wind had risen again, and was scattering a few flakes of snow—she was an attractive young person, such as foolish young men will turn round to look at for the second time, and thereby bring themselves, deservedly, against lamp-posts and pillar-letter-boxes. As if to preserve her fellow-creatures from such mischances, however, Miss Selwood dropped her veil as soon as she got clear of Moor Street, and entered an omnibus bound for the City.

The establishment in Paulet Street, of course, was closed, but she felt no hesitation in ringing at the private bell. She had naturally no *mauvaise honte*, and, had it been otherwise, the motives that were actuating her were too powerful and pressing to admit of irresolution. She had always despised and

disliked her mistress, though she had ' put up
with her ' hitherto for the sake of wages and
perquisites ; but the insulting words used by
Lady Pargiter on the previous day had sunk
deep and rankled ; and, eager for revenge,
the opportunity of wreaking it, not only with
impunity, but, as she anticipated, to her own
great advantage, had now arrived to her.

The door was opened by Mr. Brail himself, which she justly considered to be a good
sign. It was evident that even the fact of
her visit was considered too important to be
entrusted to servants. At the same time, she
was fully resolved not to be fobbed off with
Mr. Brail, who had already endeavoured, in
vain, to persuade her to confide her business
to his ear.

Mr. Signet is within, I reckon,' said she,
coming to a halt in the passage. ' What I
have to say must be said to him, and him
only. You understand that ? '

' Of course I do,' said Mr. Brail, with
tender politeness. ' You mean to deal with
principals only, and quite right—only prin-

cipals must be protected.' He wagged his head and pursed his lips, and pointed over his left shoulder to the ' parlour' door.

' I don't know what you mean,' said Miss Selwood bluntly. She had as many airs and graces at her command as most of her sex— indeed, in this respect, she was considerably above the average ; but she knew better than to waste them—upon a policeman.

' Well, the fact is, my dear,' continued Mr. Brail, no whit discomposed by his fair companion's brusqueness, ' you are one of those few young women who think too lightly of their personal attractions ; and to tell the honest truth, Mr. Signet's afraid of you. You wouldn't hurt him, of course— not you ; you wouldn't hurt anybody, if you could help it.'

' Yes, I would,' said Miss Patty vindictively.

' Ay, but that's because they deserve it,' suggested the detective ; ' because they have been doing or saying cruel things ? '

' Never you mind about that,' observed

Miss Selwood, with a sudden recollection that she was showing her hand, and to a very clever player. 'You haven't told me what Mr. Signet's afraid of me about.'

'Why, because he's a bachelor, and because you are so monstrous good-looking. Queer reasons, you will say, for his refusal to see you alone' ['Get away with you!' said Patty scornfully]; 'but so it is. The fact is'—here he sank his voice to a whisper—'the old gent is engaged to be married, and the party as is a-going to have him is that jealous that his eyes wouldn't be safe in his head if she ever come to know as he was shut up with you alone on this Sunday morning. And I don't blame her,' added Mr. Brail, with a frankness which we fear can hardly be set down in mitigation of his previous 'tarradiddles.'

'Do you mean to say that his young woman is to be present while I speak to him?' inquired Miss Selwood, with indignation.

'Not a bit of it; no, he wouldn't stand

that. " But if she's so desperate lovely, Mr.
Brail, as you describe," says she (for I was
fool enough to let out about it), "mother
must be there—that I insist upon." Then I
said, " I'll be your mother, miss ; " and so
we contrived to get over her, for I knew
you wouldn't object to *me,* my dear,' added
Mr. Brail with confidence.

'Well, I do object; though if it must
be, it must be. But you won't find two
heads better than one in getting the advantage of me, if that's what you're after.' As
that and nothing else was most distinctly
what he had been ' after ' in making the
arrangement in question, it was creditable in
Mr. Brail that he only expressed unstinted
approbation at the shrewdness which had
thus unmasked him.

'Well, that's a good un, Miss Selwood,
that is—if you never say another. When a
girl is so smart as you, it makes one wish
as one wasn't an old man—or leastways,
what is more to the purpose, wasn't tacked
to an old woman—which is my case. Just

walk this way, and mind the step. Mr. Signet,'—this he said as he ushered her into what had been poor Matthew's room—'here's Miss Selwood from Moor Street, as I told you of.'

'I am delighted to see you, miss,' said Mr. Signet. 'Pray sit down.'

Mr. Brail behind them shook his head sedately. 'He don't understand gals, *he* don't,' was the reflection passing through his brain.

'You have come, as I understand,' continued the jeweller, with an air half conciliatory, half patronising, 'to give us some information respecting these missing diamonds?'

'I am not aware as I ever said so,' observed Miss Selwood coldly. 'Some people, however, are so clever that they know a party's business better than the party do herself.'

'The young lady is alluding to me,' observed Mr. Brail playfully. 'I only understood, sir, that she had got something to

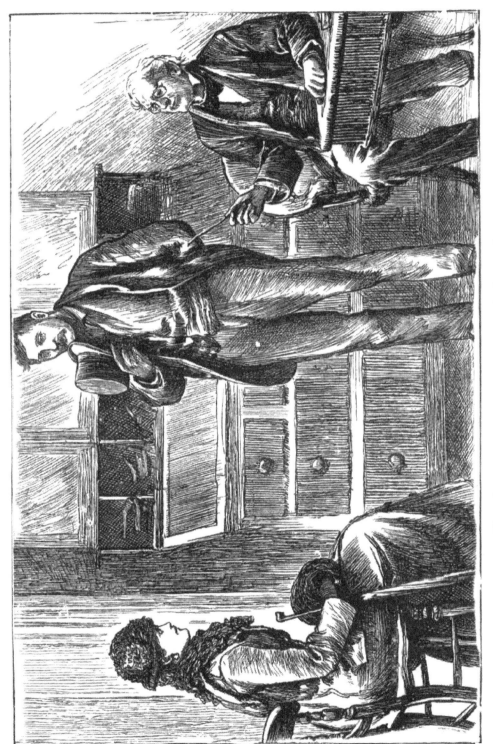

'You know aught de min' ue aun informatiou?'

say respecting Lady Pargiter's share in this mysterious matter.'

'Right you are,' observed Miss Patty, nodding her head approvingly ; 'that's the woman you have to squeeze for information. You must squeeze her pretty tight to get it.'

'I shouldn't think she was a very soft one,' hazarded Mr. Brail.

'Soft ! She hasn't got a soft spot about her—except, may be, her *'ed,'* exclaimed Patty contemptuously. 'It was precious green of her to let me see——'

'You were about to say something illustrative of Lady Pargiter's want of caution,' observed the jeweller sweetly ; for Patty had stopped herself with a scared look, much as a horseman pulls up suddenly at the edge of a chalk-pit and cranes over it. She had evidently been on the verge of letting out some secret.

'Was I ? I forgot,' said Patty cunningly. 'My mistress wants a good many things as is of more account than caution— a heart, for one thing.'

'Then you needn't be afraid of hurting her feelings,' suggested Mr. Brail. 'That's one comfort.'

'Quite the contrary,' returned Miss Selwood implacably. 'If I knew how to hurt her feelings I would; as it is, I can only hurt her pocket—rich as she is, she'll feel *that*.'

'You're a good judge of human nature, Miss Selwood,' observed the jeweller.

'I don't know about that,' she replied tartly; not that she was annoyed with her present company, but embittered by the thoughts within her. 'I am a human creature, however, like anybody else; though if you knew how some folks have treated me, you wouldn't think it.'

'She doesn't treat other people particularly well,' remarked Mr. Signet, calling to mind her ladyship's behaviour in that very room when they differed about the value of the *parure*.

'But this young lady's case is a particularly hard one,' observed Mr. Brail; 'exposed as she must be to her ladyship's ill-humour

day and night, and always having to be civil
and respectful.'

'Yes, that's it,' assented Miss Selwood
eagerly; 'I've sometimes felt inclined to cut
my tongue out for saying such smooth things
to her, when all the time I've been longing
to wring her neck. If you could hear what
she says of *you* sometimes, Mr. Signet, and
especially just lately, you'd feel something of
what I feel. I don't remember, indeed, as
she ever called you a swine.'

'Well, I hope not, my dear madam,'
interposed Mr. Signet.

'But "cheat" and "thief" are every-
day terms with her.'

'Lady Pargiter calls me a cheat and a
thief, does she?' inquired the jeweller
grimly.

'Oh, all that, and a lot more. You were
a cheat ever since you wouldn't give her
something she wanted—I don't know what
it was—but she called here about it——'

'*I* remember,' said Mr. Signet.

'It was when you wouldn't give her

her price for these very diamonds,' observed Mr. Brail. When a witness was discursive he never cut him short in full flow, but would dexterously direct him into the desired channel.

'Ah, that explains it!' continued the waiting-maid. 'She's always been hankering after turning 'em into money. Long ago she told me it would be a good job if the diamonds were lost or stolen, since you would then have to pay more for them than you would ever give if you bought them outright.'

Mr. Signet glanced at Mr. Brail, but that gentleman's gaze was fixed upon the cuckoo-clock with a look of such innocence and placidity that one would have thought it reminded him of spring time and his boyhood's years.

'And I remember,' continued Patty, 'that we agreed what a pity it was she couldn't have her cake and eat it too; that is, that she couldn't keep the jewels and yet receive the money for them.'

'Ah!' ejaculated Mr. Signet. It was but a monosyllable, but it spoke volumes. Again he looked towards Mr. Brail, and this time with positive resentment. It was monstrous that he should not be keeping his ears open while such revelations were being made. If you have ever been frightened out of your wits by a ghost, with an unbelieving bedfellow beside you who wouldn't wake and was sure to call you a fool in the morning, you can appreciate Mr. Signet's feelings at his companion's apparent unconcern.

'Then that's the very thing she planned!' exclaimed he with vehemence. 'Lady Pargiter has got the diamonds, and yet wants to make me pay for them.'

'I never said that,' observed Miss Selwood promptly.

'Of course not,' interposed Mr. Brail, taking out his handkerchief and delicately dusting the cuckoo, as that glittering bird was affirming it to be exactly noon; 'that is only Mr. Signet's own opinion: this is a free country, and he has a right to express it—in confidence.   There are circumstances, moreover, that tend to corroborate this view. You know a Mr. Harvey, I believe ?'

'Well, what then ?   Of course I know him.   He is Lady Pargiter's head footman.'

'And as fine a young fellow as ever I saw,' observed Mr. Brail. 'A man too, I should say, who would tell the truth; and yet he made a statement to me which—if the word of a certain lady of title is to be believed—is a falsehood.   He said that he himself had been sent after Mr. Matthew Helston's cab on that snowy Friday morning, which she denies.'

'I know it.   She was a fool to tell such a lie; but she has done more foolish things— and worse—than that.'

'And you are come to tell us about them,' said Mr. Brail—'for a consideration?'

'Well—yes—or, since you put it so plainly, for two con derations. I want Lady Pargiter prosecuted—punished—*punished*— that above all things; do you understand?'

'We'll do that with the greatest pleasure,' said Mr. Signet, with an alacrity that almost equalled the other's vehemence.

'Supposing we get the ground to go upon,' observed Mr. Brail cautiously.

'And of course I shall want some money down,' added Miss Selwood.

'For value received?' remarked the Detective drily. 'Why, that seems fair enough.—Now, what have you got to tell us?'

'That's very fine,' returned the young lady; 'but supposing I did tell you, and you were to turn round and say, perhaps, "Thank you"—or not even that—who would be the fool then?'

'But supposing we gave you the money first, my dear—say ten pounds—or even twenty pounds' (for Patty had glanced at him with great contempt), 'and you told us something that we knew already, or which was of no practical service to us, don't you think that would be rather hard on *us*?'

'You're big enough and strong enough

—you two—to take it back again,' urged Miss Selwood : ' whereas, if I once part with my secret—that is, the whole of it—I could never get it back from you : I should be done for.'

' I have said she was smart, but smart's no word for her,' said Mr. Brail to the cuckoo. ' Why, the Attorney-General couldn't have stated a case neater.'

' The twenty pounds shall be paid you,' chimed in Mr. Signet.

' I must have a hundred,' said Miss Selwood.   It was plain that the jeweller would have consented to this, had not the Detective interposed.

' Look here, my dear,' he said; ' I can't allow my employer to throw away his money by the pailful because it is your sweet pretty face as asks him to do it; when we get to three figures we mean business, into which the gentler feelings cannot be permitted to enter.   It seems to me that it would be fair to both parties that they should sign some sort of contract.'

'The amount to be paid to be contingent on the value of the information received,' added Mr. Signet, as his contribution to this proposal.

'You are talking gibberish,' said Miss Selwood bluntly. 'As to signing, I'll put my name to nothing, lest Lady Pargiter should come to know of it. You don't know what that woman is, or what she might do in her tantrums. Pay me down a hundred pounds, and I'll tell you something.'

'Something that will put us in the way of finding the diamonds?' said Mr. Brail.

'I don't promise you that; but it will be something that will prevent you from having to pay for them.'

'That is sufficient,' said Mr. Signet; he opened a desk and took from it twenty crisp new five-pound notes, and placed them in the girl's hand.

'I don't like the look of 'em,' observed Patty dubiously. 'I never saw no fippund notes so clean as this.'

'It's all right,' said Mr. Brail. 'We

don't make 'em here, I do assure you.—Now, what's your tip?'

'Well, what I have got to tell you about them diamonds is this—though if you had been half sharp you might have guessed it yourself—do you suppose Lady Pargiter is the kind of woman to let grass grow under her feet, and not have sent to you for her money the very next morning after the jewels disappeared, unless there was a very strong reason against it? The reason is as she has not got Helston's receipt for 'em.'

The jeweller looked inquiringly at the detective, and this time Mr. Brail returned his glance.

'The young woman's right enough so far, you may depend on't,' he replied. 'And we ought to have guessed it.'

'But where is Mr. Helston—and the diamonds?' exclaimed the jeweller.

'I don't know; leastways, if I did, that wouldn't affect the value of what I have told you. Now, if my lady writes to you for the money—which she won't dare to do, however—you have only to say she has no claim upon you. I should like to see her face when she gets that answer.—Good morning, gentlemen.'

Without hurry, yet with a swift and confident step, the young lady left the room, and passed into the street. Mr. Signet would have barred the way, but Mr. Brail prevented him. 'Let her go,' he said; 'don't set her against us. It's good to have a friend in the enemy's camp.'

'But she knows all about the diamonds and Helston's disappearance; did you not hear her say, " leastways, if I did know "?'

'Yes; but that was an afterthought of her own to increase her value in our eyes. She said plump enough "I don't know" to begin with. She has good reasons for knowing that there is no receipt, but I don't think she knows much more. What she has told—added to Rutherford's testimony—is worth a great deal to us. Though she couldn't have brought her pig to a better market, she might have sold it at a higher price.'

Curiously enough, Miss Patty Selwood's thoughts as she took her way westward were running on the same subject which Mr. Brail had taken for his metaphor.

'A swine is a pig,' she was saying to herself: 'nobody ever had to pay so much for a pig—or the use of a pig's name—as you will have to pay, my lady.'

CHAPTER XXIX.

WRITING FOR THE PRESS.

THE cool head is the great winner in the game of life. To it fall all the prizes of the material sort : money ; good position in the law and commerce ; and generally what reputation, of the respectable kind, can con- fer. In rare instances, it even attains the highest honours. These make up to its possessor for a lack of enjoyments which by the nature of the case are denied to him. For Love, for Friendship, for almost all kinds of social pleasure, a man must be more or less impulsive : if he begins to calculate about them, they are lost to him. The Poet has delights which the Financier, though he has made millions, can never share. I am not, of course, speaking of the 'philosophic mind,' which, to say truth, very few of us, whether poets or otherwise, ever attain to, but of the order of man whom his friends term philosophic; the world in general a ' cool head;' and his enemies a ' cool hand.' He is almost always prosperous. If he be not, he is of all men the most miserable; for to Prosperity he has pinned himself, and what would be his position with the pin through him and nothing to stick it to!

Mr. Signet was pre-eminently a man of this class, but not altogether by nature. He had had impulses in his time (he had some even now, as we know), but the circumstances of his life and trade had sobered him. He knew how to wait. Men say of a wealthy man that he can ' afford' to wait— to hold on to dropping stock till it rises, or to depreciated goods till they are in demand again; but in nine cases out of ten what has helped him to become rich, has been a natural aptitude for biding his time. As compared with their less prudently constituted fellows, these men are like bill-discounters who have to deal with spendthrifts. It is only the

cleverest of them, however, who are aware
how many men are eagerly desirous to get
matters settled out of hand, even at a loss,
and to have done with bother. Bother does
not affect *them*, and they are therefore fortu
nately ignorant of the jar and jangle that it
causes in the whole harmony of Being in
others : otherwise they would take even
greater advantage of them than they do.

Lady Pargiter was by no means what is
generally understood by the phrase 'a creature of impulse;' she inherited the caution
and total absence of sentiment of her father
the money-lender; but she lacked his
heavenly temper. No ill-behaviour of his
clients ever roused him to passion; one man
whom the exigencies of the case compelled
him to send to prison (though he had already
repaid his original loan twice over) once spat
in his face. Mr. Ingot was not a Christian,
yet no word of anger crossed his lips. You
would never have discovered that he had
been insulted, unless you had been a Taxing
Master and had had that particular Bill of

Costs relating to the offender under your consideration. But Lady Pargiter, besides an ungovernable temper, had been very rich for years, which is a great hindrance to patience. The most engaging of epicures once observed to me in a moment of confidence (it was after some canvas-backed ducks), 'I like everything good, and very often, and a great deal of it.' And Lady Pargiter, though not in matters relating to the table, had the same tastes. She liked her own way always, and to have it at once.

It was this difference of character between her ladyship and Mr. Signet that made the combat between them over Matthew Helston's missing body so much more equal than it looked to be. For, at the first blush, her ladyship would have appeared to have both legal and moral right upon her side.

Mr. Signet's confidential agent had disappeared with her diamonds, for which Mr. Signet was therefore responsible. And if she had not been conscious of at least one flaw in her armour, she would without doubt

have struck the first blow. Her not having
done so had indeed to Mr. Signet, who knew
her character, appeared strange, though,
unlike Mr. Brail, he could not allow it to
have been so strange that it ought to have
suggested the reason. But now her whole
conduct was explicable enough, even to her
having inspired the paragraph in the morning paper which had so deeply offended him.
Unable to restrain her impatience, yet not
daring to demand the money from him
point-blank, she had used that device to
draw from him an acknowledgment of his
indebtedness; and, but for Rutherford's evidence, might have succeeded. It was likely
enough that Mr. Signet should have communicated with her, and if so he could hardly
have expressed his sorrow for what had happened, and his hopes that the jewels might
be recovered, without admitting his responsibility. But now nothing was further from
his thoughts. If he had decided upon
fighting a desperate cause, with nothing but
the cabman's evidence to back it, how much

more was he ready to do battle now! For
not only, supposing Miss Selwood's information was correct, had he discovered the weak
point of her ladyship's case, but was more
convinced than ever that she had the diamonds in her possession; it might have been
by bribing Helston, or even by murdering
him, but 'somehow or other,' he said to
himself, 'that woman has got them.' For a
long-headed, cautious man of business, it
was extraordinary how he loathed Lady
Pargiter; his confidence in Patty was perhaps
as much owing to her evident hatred of her
mistress as to the assistance her testimony
promised to him. The accusations which
her ladyship had been so imprudent as to
make against him had aroused his deepest
resentment, for if there was one thing on
which he prided himself (and there were
many) it was his honesty. This sentiment
was quite apart from the sensitiveness with
which Sabey resented the least slur upon her
husband's honour; he had the pride of the
British tradesman, in that he had paid his

way, and made it ; had not been bankrupt ;
and had never, or hardly ever, taken advantage of a fellow-creature, except in the
way of business. Moreover—and this he
plumed himself upon more than all—he had
refrained from doing dishonest acts on several
occasions when he might have done them
with impunity. Such slanders as Lady Pargiter's were not only galling to a mind thus
conscious of its own rectitude, but threatened
his credit. Her ladyship's immense wealth
gave her great influence ; but, on the other
hand, reflected Mr. Signet, if she was only
a little more imprudent, would make her
well worth ' shooting at ' in an action for
damages.

On that Sunday afternoon Mr. Brail and
his employer had a long discussion upon the
plan of the coming campaign ; for that there
would be a fight with Lady Pargiter they
took for granted. The detective was for
remaining quite quiet, or, as I am sorry to say,
he had the discourtesy to express it, for
' giving the woman plenty of rope ; ' but Mr.

Signet was eager for action. In the end a compromise was effected : it was decided that no direct attack should be made against the enemy, but a flank movement, and with such a show of force as might draw him from his entrenchments. A paragraph was to be written to the newspapers taking quite another view of the disappearance of the diamonds than that which had been already made public. Mr. Signet accordingly retired to an upstairs apartment, and devoted himself for some hours to composition : it was a line he was not used to, but for which in his secret heart he imagined himself to have a natural bent ; only, he was too modest to compose in the presence of another person. Give him solitude, however—and a dictionary—and the result was one with which he was generally well content.

On the present occasion he elaborated quite a treatise upon the annals of his respectable firm : how it had begun in obscurity, progressed through integrity and attention to business, and culminated in 'one of the largest establishments connected with jewels and the precious metals in the City of London.' Then he described the 'system' on which the establishment worked, and showed it to be faultless. One of the precautions it took was only to employ assistants after the pattern of the members of the firm themselves—namely, of the most unblemished character. Under such circumstances it was impossible, he argued, that Messrs. Star and Signet could be morally responsible for any loss whatever: nevertheless, they were always prepared to accept their responsibilities, however gigantic, which the extent of their resources easily enabled them to do. As to the mysterious disappearance, however, of Lady Pargiter's diamonds, a contemporary had fallen into the error of supposing that Messrs. Star and Signet admitted a liability which in fact lay altogether elsewhere, as they had written and other evidence to prove.

The space occupied by the missing man in this eloquent composition, notwithstanding that it was a little long and decidedly discursive, was about three lines ; nor were the jewels themselves much dwelt upon—with the ingenious design of hinting that their loss was Lady Pargiter's business ; but as a monograph on the House of Star and Signet, it was superb.

Mr. Brail's face said so, as his employer read out the rolling periods in a sonorous voice.

'Beautiful, beautiful !' he said, when the reading was finished. 'The style is—dear me—' he looked round, as if for a fitting adjective, and his eye, lighting upon a ticket appended to an Aphrodite in frosted silver, found what it sought—'very chaste. I had no idea, sir, you possessed the literary gift. But it won't do for the newspapers.'

'Won't do?' cried Mr. Signet, the expression of his face changing from gratified pride to an irritation that was almost truculent. 'What's the matter with it ?'

'Nothing, my dear sir : in its own way it's perfect ; but for a newspaper it's too good.'

Mr. Signet's brow relaxed: he himself thought that there was a waste of force in composing such an essay for a penny daily; but still, a man of genius can't suit his style to the lower classes: moreover, he wanted to see it in print.

'It's all true, and it's all very pretty,' continued his critic: 'and you needn't waste it, you know: it will do admirably for a Christmas advertisement' [Mr. Signet shuddered]; 'but it shows too much the source from which it comes. Apart from its excellence (which itself, my dear sir, would betray its author), it has too much of Star and Signet in it. To use a vulgar image, it smells of the shop.'

'Smells of the shop?' repeated Mr. Signet, putting the manuscript mechanically to his nose. 'Not a bit of it. You would not have me write about my jewels without speaking of myself?'

'Certainly not; not about *your* jewels; but we are concerning ourselves with Lady Pargiter's jewels. It is she, we contend, who has lost them, or got them : you should have condoled with her, just as the other fellow did with you.'

'I couldn't do it,' said Mr. Signet candidly. 'She's a thief and a liar.'

'Just so,' answered the other cheerfully; 'but it is injudicious to prove it by praising our own truth and integrity. Put it on Matthew Helston's shoulders. Adopt a tone of virtuous indignation. Why should a man " poor but honest " be suspected of a crime, because the person who has suffered—or, rather, has apparently suffered—is rich and powerful? It is not worth our while, let them understand, to defend ourselves in this matter, but we feel that something is owing to the character of a tried and faithful servant—a man we have trusted with untold gold, and priceless articles of *vertu*. I am no scholar, like you, Mr. Signet, but I know the Public and what tickles 'em, and while you were upstairs I just ventured to throw together my own views of how the thing should run, and here they are. Perhaps you would kindly put 'em into proper shape.'

The few sentences the detective had jotted down in his note-book were certainly not to be compared to the ornate production of Mr. Signet; but they did not lack a certain vigour, which was the more credit-able to him considering that he didn't believe a word he wrote. For he still secretly stuck to his first view that Helston had made off with the jewels.

'Dear me,' said Mr. Signet, 'this is very bald—and—um, commonplace. "Respect-able young man," "well connected," "stain of reproach," "confidence of employer." However, I dare say I can make something of it—"wreck of a household "—" suspend their opinion."—That seems all right.'

'Then you can conclude,' said Mr. Brail, ' with your own admirable hit against Lady Pargiter.'

Mr. Signet nodded adhesion; he was glad that all his labour was not to be thrown away, and he was beginning to be pleased with this new and improved version of the affair for a reason that even the detective could not have fathomed. His thus putting publicly forward his confidence in Helston's integrity could not but be gratifying to Amy Thurlow.

CHAPTER XXX.

AN INTERVIEW WITH THE LADIES.

RICH men who can afford to neglect their business, or idle men who have none, have exceptional opportunities (though it does not appear that they universally take advantage of them) of cultivating the domestic affections. It is curious, when one comes to think of it, what a very small portion of his life a man in business, or in one of the professions (if he practises as well as professes), passes in the society of his wife and children. He sees them at breakfast-time, and that is in many cases absolutely the only time that he sets eyes upon his little ones, for he does not come home to his late dinner till they are gone to bed. In the case of his grown-up progeny he dines and spends the evening with them—and, except on Sundays, that is all the intercourse between them. A vast deal more of his time—that is, of his life—is spent with Tom, Dick, and Harry in the Law Courts, or (I regret to add) during his afternoon rubbers at the club, than in the society of his nearest and dearest.

Tom and Dick are scarcely aware, perhaps, that he *is* married; and, on the other hand, his family are not much interested in Tom and Dick. He passes, in fact, two separate existences, though we are in the habit of speaking and thinking of him as if he had but one. Nature, I think, is kind in this matter, or one would fear that the absent Paterfamilias would be looked upon by his offspring more as a mere Bread-winner, and less as a Father, than is the case with the male parent who can afford to stop at home and cultivate the home affections. The stay-at-home, however, fortunately doesn't always cultivate them. I have known families who complain that dear papa has no occupation of his own, and therefore worries himself (i.e. insists on

meddling) about matters of the house. We
all know what a hunting man is within doors
during a hard frost; and think of having an
infliction of the same sort *always*! These
things no doubt tend to equalise matters;
and may be set down on the *per contra* side.
The man of business and the barrister can
scarcely become unpopular at home through
being too much there.

In the case of the little household in
Cavendish Grove, Uncle Stephen was generally to be found on the nest, while poor
Matthew, before he left it altogether in so
mysterious a fashion, had to forage far away
for food from morn to eve; and the same
fate, though he had no household at present,
was Mr. Frank Barlow's. On Sundays, of
course, that gentleman was at leisure, and I
am afraid Mr. Signet took this fact into his
calculations in deferring to bring to No. 7
the tidings he had received from Miss Selwood, until Monday. I cannot persuade
myself that it was sheer respect for the Sab-
bath, when he had passed its morning in

interviewing that young lady, and its afternoon in literary composition.

He called about eleven o'clock, when all
really hardworking lawyers have been in
their cobwebs for an hour, and most of them
have caught a fly or two, and asked boldly
for Miss Thurlow. He was shown into the
dining-room, where that young lady at once
joined him ; he did not perhaps quite understand that it was for Matthew's sake she
could not afford to lose a moment, but set
down her promptness to a motive more com-
plimentary to himself. Her welcome, however, though perfectly genuine—for how
could she be otherwise than eager to hear
his news ?—was far from demonstrative. She
did not return the pressure of his hand, and
looked so grave in answer to his ' My *dear*
Miss Thurlow,' and the sympathetic manner
which accompanied it, that one less conscious
of his own merits, and of the happiness he
proposed to confer, might have imagined that
she designed to reprove him. She had cause
enough for gravity, poor soul, as they all had

in that house; but her air was designedly
more distant than it had been on the last
occasion.   This was because she had assured
Mr. Barlow that nothing should induce her
to alter her behaviour to Mr. Signet.

On the previous day they had had a long
discussion about him, in the course of which
Mr. Barlow had said some hard things of the
worthy jeweller.   He had called him a self-
seeking, coarse-grained, grasping fellow, who
—notwithstanding any pretensions he might
make to good feeling—had nothing in view
but his own ends.

'I don't think he is grasping,' Amy had
rejoined, without any reference to the other
charges; 'on the contrary, considering that
he has so much money, and has made most
of it himself, he appears to me to be rather
careless of expenditure.'

'He is ostentatious enough, no doubt.'

'No, I don't think he is ostentatious,
Frank.'

Her reading of Mr. Signet's character was
so far correct: he was fond of money—that

is to say, he had the British trader's delight in turning the nimble ninepence—but he was too shrewd to be avaricious. If he did not know that *miser* was the Latin for miserable, he felt that they were synonymous terms. Schemes for scraping and saving were abhorrent to him. He gave employés excellent wages, and upon the whole they liked him. And he treated himself to anything to which he took a fancy, regardless of its price. He was about to measure his purse against Lady Pargiter's quite as much from his personal dislike of her as with a view of evading his responsibility with respect to the jewels, though indeed he firmly believed she had got them.

It is not to be supposed that, even yet, Mr. Frank Barlow was jealous of a man double his own age and little more than half his height, but his pretensions, which he by this time well understood, were naturally offensive to him. It was indeed to the last degree impudent of the man to entertain them, knowing as he did that Miss Thurlow was engaged; but, on the other hand, he had never made any actual proposal to her; and, if he did, Amy had an all-sufficient answer to it. Under other circumstances, no doubt, she would have taken measures for dismissing him at once: but it seemed monstrous to her, after that communication of Mr. Durham's to him, that the jeweller should still entertain such hopes; and his aid and countenance were just now so necessary to poor Matthew, even though it were only to his memory. Moreover, the whole case lay in Mr. Signet's hands, and on him they were dependent for those tidings which, to one at least in that household, had become the only thing to which her ears were open.

'I will not make an enemy of Mr. Signet, if I can help it,' Amy had said; not with vehemence, for she showed no sign of 'temper,' but with a resolution that not even a lover's remonstrance could shake.

'I don't ask you to be rude to him,' returned Mr. Barlow, rather weakly, for he himself was a good deal 'put out;' 'but you ought not to encourage him.'

'Encourage him, Frank?'

There was an indignation in her eyes as well as her tone which should have made the young lawyer repent having used so strong a term; but he prided himself on never making any allegation without proofs —nor even then, if it was actionable.

'You are wearing the ring he gave you on your finger, Amy,' he said. 'You are well aware that at one time he had the intention of proposing to you—yes, you are; if you could not gather it from his own conduct to yourself, his behaviour when poor Matthew told him you were engaged to me put that beyond a doubt. And being purse-proud, and not a gentleman, nor anything like it, he still thinks he has a chance.'

Amy made a gesture of disbelief, that had also something of disgust in it.

'Supposing even that you are right, Frank, which I utterly refuse to believe,' she said, 'you have still to explain how I have encouraged him.'

'He calls on you personally, and you do not refuse to see him ; you would have seen him alone yesterday if I had not prevented it. His manner towards you—his affectation of sympathy, that is—is most impertinent.'

'But why should he not feel sympathy with us ?' she urged ; 'a heart of stone might feel it.'

'Then let him be sympathetic with *me*. Let him talk to *me* with his hand upon his heart, and in a voice broken with emotion. It's all a piece of acting.'

'Still, you have not yet come to your charge against me of encouraging him.'

'Well, you encourage him by pretending to believe his sympathy to be genuine ; by seeing him alone ; by talking to him in a confidential manner. I should wish—if it is necessary to see the man at all—that your manner to him should be altered.'

'My dear Frank,' said Amy, speaking very gently, 'I must see Mr. Signet when he comes, because he is the bearer of tidings which have a vital interest for me. To please you—though I think it cruel and unjust of you to entertain such suspicions of him, under the circumstances in which my poor sister and I are placed; any man with a heart would as soon think of making love over a death-bed—to please you I will not see Mr. Signet alone; but he has been on the whole both kind and considerate to us, and I cannot make him the ill return of being uncivil to him. I see nothing to find fault with in my manner towards him, and I shall maintain it.'

And that was why she was so cold and grave to Mr. Signet when he called the next day.

That gentleman, however, put this down as a consequence of the domestic calamity, which each hour of course was rendering more deep and hopeless.

'And how is your poor sister, Miss Thurlow?'

'Her state is most distressing; but on

hearing you were here she at once expressed a wish to see you. Will you kindly come with me ?' and she moved towards the door, which at her entrance she had not closed behind her.

'Well, I wanted to say a few words to you first and alone. I have the strangest news to communicate to you concerning Lady Pargiter.'

'That will interest my sister, Mr. Signet, equally with myself. Be good enough to step this way.'

Her face was flushed with the recollection of her promise to Frank—that is, of the reason why she was declining to let Mr. Signet speak with her alone ; but her voice was very firm. It was impossible to mistake her object, and Mr. Signet set it down to a last desperate attempt upon the young woman's part to resist his fascinations. A struggle of this kind was under the circumstances only to have been expected. There were certain ties to be sundered ; he did not like her the less for not dropping into his hands like a ripe peach. Moreover, he found it necessary to obey her, and followed her at once into the parlour where Sabey was sitting, fronting the window as usual, with some baby-clothes upon her lap. It was curious, and very sad, to see the change those few days of misery had wrought in her. Her figure, always slight, had become almost emaciated. Her youth was gone, its brightness and buoyancy exchanged for a certain haggard keenness—such as is generally to be seen only in the vicious and the degraded; only her eyes redeemed her from any such associations. Naturally large, they had now attained abnormal dimensions; or perhaps the shrinking of the face made it appear so, while the expression of them was pitiful to the last degree: 'homes of silent prayer' they might well indeed be called; but with a certain look of resolve in them, also, which is not the usual accompaniment of religious resignation.

'It is very kind of you, Mr. Signet, to come to us so often,' she said; and the jeweller noticed that her voice, though low, had a greater clearness than on the last occasion. 'Your news is the only news that has any interest for us now.'

'I only wish it were better, my dear Mrs. Helston. Still'—for he noticed the little colour in her cheeks paled away at once—'I have at least no worse news for you than on Saturday. It chiefly relates to Lady Pargiter. Your husband and I always took the same view of her ladyship's character; but nothing that we thought of her can come up to what I have now cause to believe her capable of. Conceive her attempting to hold me responsible for her diamonds, without even possessing my agent's receipt for them. From information received—— However, to such friends as yourself and your excellent sister, I may say exactly what has occurred.'

Then he repeated to them the revelation made by Miss Patty Selwood. When all was told, and perceiving that Mrs. Helston—to whom he had mainly addressed himself—was by no means so moved by the recital as he had expected, he turned to her sister.

'Mrs. Helston does not appear to comprehend the enormous importance that the absence of this receipt may be to us?'

'Nay, rather, Mr. Signet, she does not—nor, I confesss, do I—perceive its bearing upon the disappearance of her husband.'

The jeweller—whom the glitter of the diamonds had for the time, as it were, blinded to this other particular—hastened to repair his mistake.

'Then let me explain that at once,' he said. 'The fact I speak of has a very strong though indirect relation to your domestic calamity. It makes Rutherford's evidence against Lady Pargiter of much more weight; it points to her guilty knowledge of the robbery, and therefore by implication of what has become of Mr. Helston, and in this light it is hopeful.'

'In what respect?' inquired Amy.

'Well; though she may have stolen the

diamonds, it is unlikely that she would have gone to the length of——of doing any bodily harm to Mr. Helston. She has probably only put him out of the way. I mean that since there must needs be some guilty person in this matter, it is better if it turns out to be her ladyship than any ordinary criminal who might stick at nothing. It is this reflection that gives me such satisfaction in her waiting-maid's statement.'

'But it is incredible,' said Amy, 'that even Lady Pargiter—or indeed any woman— could have——'

'Oh, I beg your pardon; it's just *like* a woman,' interrupted Mr. Signet; 'or rather, I should say,' he added, with a sudden remembrance of the sex of his auditors, 'it is just like the conduct of a person unused to commit this class of crimes. Her course of conduct has been so audacious, and so careless of the consequences. She sends her own servant to recall the cab (which, remember, she has since denied); she persuades Mr. Helston to remain under her roof on the pretence of hospitality, and then causes him to be deprived by force of that which had been entrusted to his charge; but, being honest and faithful, he refuses—no matter under what pressure—to furnish her with the receipt which constitutes her legal claim.'

'But should not Matthew have given her the receipt before he quitted the house the first time?' observed Amy.

'A very judicious remark,' observed Mr. Signet; 'the very one that Mr. Brail, my detective, himself made when I suggested my view of the case. Yes, she had his receipt no doubt; but, somehow or other, Mr. Helston must have had the opportunity of destroying it afterwards, when he perceived her wicked intentions. That is only a bare supposition, of course; but the whole affair is at present guesswork. Nothing that we can suppose is, at all events, more improbable than what has actually occurred; and my explanation of the matter accounts for both the absence of the receipt and the disappearance of Mr. Helston. As to the

latter—which is, of course, our main consideration—I am unable to dismiss from my
mind the circumstance that your excellent
husband was personally obnoxious to Lady
Pargiter. This, though it may not absolutely
account for everything, may be a factor in
the case. She may have attempted to bribe
him ; there may have been a quarrel ; and,
being of an ungovernable temper and utterly
unscrupulous, she may have been driven further than she intended.'

'Do you mean to suggest,' said Sabey in
hollow tones, 'that this woman has *murdered*
my husband ?'

'My dear madam, nothing of the kind.
You alarm me above measure, and make me
regret having reposed my confidence in you.
To one person—that is to say, without a
witness—one can say anything ; that is why
I was so anxious to speak with Miss Thurlow
alone upon this matter. I hope another
time that she will understand that I have
a reason for what I ask. But before a witness—that is to say, when you are both

present—it is unadvisable to open one's heart too unreservedly. Not that Lady Pargiter has any right to complain of my saying anything. The infamous accusations of dishonesty that she has made against myself and Mr. Helston——'

'When ? Where ?' inquired Sabey with sudden eagerness ; her liquid eyes aglow, like the phosphorescent gleam of some ocean lake.

'She made them to Mr. Brail ; she made them to her waiting-maid ; she caused them, without doubt, to find their way on Saturday into print. By-the-by, I have another newspaper paragraph to show you that concerns us all, Mrs. Helston.'

'Let me see it—give it to me,' she cried, with eagerness. Amy made no attempt to stop her : the infamous suggestions against her husband's honour of which she was already in possession had had, as Uncle Stephen had predicted, by no means a bad effect upon Sabey. Strange to say, indeed, they might be said to have had a good effect : they had substituted for her brooding, an indignant, almost defiant, frame of mind; and for her despondent and despairing thoughts all sorts of schemes for vindicating his innocence, which, however vague and impracticable, were by comparison a wholesome mental pabulum. It gave her a sort of galvanic strength, and—what was of real consequence—a desire for life, though but for a single end. Even though her Matthew were lost for ever to her, she would not wish to die before she had given the lie to his detractors and cleared his memory from reproach.

'This paper takes quite a different view,' observed Mr. Signet encouragingly.

'Yes; I suppose I ought to be thankful for it,' said Sabey with a sad smile.

'The writer, at all events, meant kindly,' put in Amy, who was reading over her shoulder.

'I am sure he did,' said the jeweller, blushing; not because he had written the paragraph—for, as we know, that was not the case—but because he knew that he was producing the impression that he had done so.

'Have you brought me back Matthew's picture?' inquired Sabey softly.

'No, not to-day; yesterday was Sunday, you know—a *dies non*—I shall hope to bring it you'—here he turned to Amy— 'to-morrow.'

'My sister will be glad to have it back,' said Amy. It was very disagreeable to Mr. Signet that she would persist in avoiding any reference to herself. He was discouraged by the result of his visit altogether, though he felt that he might have made a worse impression but for his own dexterity. The indifference these women had manifested to his news about the diamonds was most extraordinary; of course they were anxious about Helston, but they seemed to have no sense of comparison. He began to think that Amy had not quite so much intelligence as he had credited her with; and yet, somehow, he did not think less of

her on that account. The tenderness of the
Dove seemed in her case preferable to the
sagacity of the Owl; and yet, with all her
quietness, he was aware that there was a
certain air of self-confidence about her—the
natural fruit, had he but known it, of inde-
pendence of character; and that also gave
him satisfaction. He felt that a woman of
that kind, if properly dressed (so he put it,
as though she had been *on* the board instead
of *at* it), would look uncommonly well at
the head of his table.

Amy did not accompany him—as on the
last occasion—to the front door, but rang
the parlour bell for the maid-servant; and
he could not but perceive that the pressure
of his hand at parting was not returned.

This wounded his self-love. Still, all
previous engagements notwithstanding, he
could scarcely conceive her refusing the sole
surviving representative of Star and Signet
if he should really condescend to propose to
her. At present he had not positively made
up his mind to do so. If Lady Pargiter's

guilt should be brought home to her, he would offer the girl his hand; but if it should turn out that Matthew Helston had absconded with the jewels, he was not sure his passion for her was so strong that it would survive her connection with disgrace.

CHAPTER XXXI.

UNCLE STEPHEN'S VIEW.

It sometimes happens, though very rarely, that some great passenger ship, bound for America or the Indies, will go down in the waste of ocean and leave not a vestige of her existence behind her; and even then in the minds of those who have had their dear ones entrusted to her treacherous keeping there is hope. She may have been delayed by contrary winds, or beaten out of her course; then when such time elapses as to forbid that supposition, it is possible—just possible—that she may have been wrecked on some out-of-the-way if not unknown coast, and her living tenants saved. But even this well-nigh desperate case affords no parallel in respect of its lack of hope to that of the sudden disappearance in the waste of London of an honest man entrusted with a great treasure. Every suggestion of common sense points to but one explanation of such a mystery. To those who believe in his integrity, he is as a dead man; and in their eyes it is better so, since otherwise he must needs be what he appears in the eyes of the world at large—a Thief.

Into the minds of Matthew Helston's wife and sister this last supposition, indeed, could never enter; but day by day the other alternative was being urged with greater force upon them. It was a sort of *peine forte et dure* of the mind; the weight upon it was increased hour by hour—' as much as they could bear,' as the old brutal statute said, ' and more.'

Sabey still took her meals—nourishment sufficient to keep life and even strength within her, for strength, she vaguely felt, might, for Matthew's sake, be required of her; but she took them in her own room. Society, even that of her own belongings, was become too much for her; to conversation, even upon the subject next her heart, she could no longer give attention. Mr. Barlow saw her every evening for a few minutes; she looked for his coming vaguely— he might be the bearer of some news. And Uncle Stephen would come and sit in silence by her side, with her little hand clasped in his, for half an hour at a time. But so cruel was her case, that friendship and sympathy had lost their power.

Both men were too honest and too wise any longer to encourage hope within her, and it was for that alone she yearned; and the visits of Mr. Signet were, for this reason, absolutely more welcome to her.

Amy's presence, on the other hand, was very precious: not from the habit of old days and their associations unconsciously working with her, but because Amy alone knew what she felt, and could, in part at least, share her sorrow. She insisted, however, on her sister's dining below stairs.

' It is hard enough for dear Uncle Stephen

as it is,' she said: 'I am very hard upon him myself——'

'He understands, darling,' put in Amy.

'I hope so, I trust so. Matthew owes him so much; tell him if I live, and if—' (she would have said, supposing her husband was not alive, but she could not frame the words)—'I will repay him with my utmost love and service; but just now, I can only think of Matthew.'

On the evening of Mr. Signet's visit, the three had a long talk together over Matthew's case. Mr. Barlow, of course, had seen the second newspaper paragraph, and brought it home with him.

He ascribed it to the mere spirit of newspaper opposition; that since one journal had taken sides with Lady Pargiter, its rival leant towards Mr. Signet's view of the case.

'I don't think the man himself could have written it,' he said; 'it is not sufficiently egotistic: he could never have kept Star and Signet out of it for so many lines.'

'We understood from Mr. Signet's manner to-day,' said Amy, using the plural by design, ' that he had, at all events, instigated the paragraph.'

' Instigated ? ' cried Uncle Stephen ; ' it's his own! I could swear to it as though I had seen his handwriting. That *mens conscia recti* of his betrays him.'

' It is not badly composed, however, for the purpose for which it is intended,' remarked Mr. Barlow, who had seen nothing inappropriate in the quotation. ' As a defence of Matthew's moral character it is of course contemptible, but it is likely enough to make Lady Pargiter show her hand.'

Uncle Stephen was about to speak, but altered his mind.

' You mean to say that there will be a lawsuit ? ' inquired Amy.

' Yes, my dear; Mr. Signet, as I understand, is resolved, supposing the waiting-maid's evidence to be trustworthy, to fight it out.'

' I did not like to mention it to him this morning,' said Amy, ' because it might look as if we thought he was not doing his best : but why does not Mr. Signet offer a reward for the recovery of the jewels?   That would surely help us.'

'Very likely,' observed Mr. Barlow cynically : 'but the question he puts to himself is, will it help *him*?   His present object is to pretend the loss of the jewels is no business of his, and whoever first offers the reward will appear to make it his business.'

'Why should not *we* offer a reward for Matthew?' said Uncle Stephen. 'That's our business, surely.'

'I have thought of that, of course,' replied Mr. Barlow, with rather a pitying air. 'But looking at the matter all round, I think we had better not do that—at least, at present.   The Police — all constituted authorities, in fact—are doing their best to elucidate the affair ; and an offer of a reward would only call more public attention to it —which is far from desirable.'

Why?' inquired Amy.

'Well, really, my dear, you astonish me

by such a question. Is not your poor brother-in-law's name bandied about already sufficiently? And yet, you may be sure, these paragraphs are but the beginning of things. If you heard, as I do, what is said in every omnibus and railway carriage——'

'I should not care what I heard,' interrupted Amy, 'if only more publicity could assist us in finding Matthew. What is the opinion of the whole world to Sabey—who is the person we have alone to consider in this matter—compared with that?'

'That sort of publicity could not assist us, Amy,' said Mr. Barlow; he spoke quietly, without the least trace of irritation, but his face showed a rising colour.

'I think—not immediately, perhaps, but very shortly—Sabey ought herself to be consulted in the matter,' observed Uncle Stephen. 'She is, as Amy says, our first consideration; and no inconvenience or distress of mind to anyone—to ourselves, for example—ought to prevent our leaving a stone unturned.'

'You will, of course, act, Mr. Durham, as you think proper,' replied the lawyer.

Nothing more, for the moment, was said on this point : but when Amy had withdrawn to join her sister, 'I hope,' said Mr. Barlow, 'you did not suppose that it was with any reference to myself—that is, with respect to the reputation of the family with which I am about to be connected—that I opposed any reward being offered with regard to Matthew?'

'Well, to say the truth, Barlow, I thought that might have weighed with you.'

'I think it did not—I hope it did not, Mr. Durham. But I confess I object to our taking any action which may be supposed to be in common with Mr. Signet. He is in my opinion pursuing a most unwarrantable and unscrupulous course. He knows that Lady Pargiter has no more possession of those diamonds than I have.'

'I certainly think it very improbable,' mused Mr. Durham.

'Improbable? It is impossible. The

notion that the woman should have stolen her own jewels is monstrous. As to the receipt—it may have been destroyed by accident; that matters not to us one fig. The question for us is not where the jewels are, but where is Matthew?'

'And what is your view?'

'I believe John Rutherford could tell us all, if he chose. He has trumped up that story about having left his fare in Moor Street. I don't believe one word of it.'

'Then you must needs believe he has murdered him?'

'I hope for the best, and in God's mercy, Mr. Durham; but that is my conviction,' answered Mr. Barlow gravely. 'There is no other way out of it.'

'There are plenty of ways out of it, my dear sir, if we had but the wit to see them,' returned Uncle Stephen. 'From all I can gather, the cabman is an honest fellow, and —which weighs with me still more—he was personally attached to Matthew. A man may murder a stranger for money, or even a blood relation whom he does not love; but not his friend. Sabey has been kind to Rutherford's wife, and he has shown himself sensible of it. He must have had both gratitude and liking to contend against. We are presupposing a monstrosity in imputing murder, under such circumstances, to such a man. Besides, he has had scores of opportunities before this one.'

'Yes; but this was the last chance, and he knew it. That some one has done it is morally certain. Do you prefer to think Lady Pargiter the murderess?'

'Don't let us use such words, Mr. Barlow, till they have been justified by the event,' said Uncle Stephen reprovingly.

'Do you think Matthew would have parted with those jewels, then, and kept his life?'

'Mr. Barlow,' returned Uncle Stephen, 'I know Matthew Helston better than you do, and certainly respect him as much. Of course I do not think that.'

'Then, in my opinion, all that we have

to hope for is this—that, since the robbery must in all probability have been committed by several persons, in time they will quarrel among themselves, and Matthew's memory will be cleared of stain.'

'That does not follow,' said Uncle Stephen. 'When M. d'Anglade was in prison, where he died, after the torture, for his supposed robbery of the Count de Montgomery, it is on record that the whole body of Paris thieves were cognisant that two of their number—Belestre and Gagnard—were the real culprits.'

'Then it appears that you are more hopeless respecting this terrible affair than even I am?'

'No: I cannot say I am without hope,' answered Uncle Stephen thoughtfully. 'I have lived too long in the world not to know how expectation is baulked, even though it be of a misfortune.'

'But you feel certain that the diamonds have been stolen?'

Mr. Durham hesitated; held his chin in

his hand, as was his habit when thinking deeply; and then slowly replied: 'Yes: we must suppose them to have been stolen.'

'Then Matthew, as you agreed with me, cannot be alive?'

'I did not say that, Barlow: in my opinion, he would not have parted with what was entrusted to him, save with his life. But they might have been forced from him. This affair is not one of alternatives— that is the view of the police, no doubt; but it is much too shallow and narrow. Ten thousand things *may* have taken place where one thing does take place. I am inclined to think that in this case something very ab- normal, and out of the policeman's beat, has happened. To Sabey and Amy—dear souls —I may have appeared indifferent: I did not wish to melt their waxen hearts by too much show of sympathy; but night and day, of late, I have thought of nothing but Matthew.'

'Then you have a theory to account for his disappearance?' exclaimed Mr. Barlow cagerly. He would have called his companion ' a very bad man of business' (meaning a 'dreamer'), but he had a genuine admiration for his abilities; and he thought it quite possible that, where practical minds were at fault, his ingenuity might supply a clue.

'Well, yes, I have. It seems wild enough, but then the whole affair is wild, and *similia similibus curantur*, as Mr. Signet would say. And, again, it is not a rose-water solution of the enigma; one cannot object to it that it makes things too pleasant. Still, it's better than murder or robbery.'

'If your explanation avoids these two horns of the dilemma, it must indeed be worth hearing,' said Mr. Barlow.

'Turn the key in the door, will you?' continued Uncle Stephen. 'I should not like even Amy to come in just now. I feel that I could not pull myself together in a moment.' The old man's face indeed showed a pain that was distressing to behold, and his voice was feeble and broken. 'You must excuse me, sir,' he said, with a certain dignity, 'but this lad is dear to me as the apple of my eye. Whatever I tell you now —whether it turns out to be the fact or otherwise—I must have your promise that it will be kept secret.'

'You may trust me, Mr. Durham: I shall regard you as a client in consultation.'

A smile flitted across Uncle Stephen's face, but only to leave it graver than before.

'I have noticed for some time,' he said, 'a certain depression in Matthew; he has been always quiet and even depressed, you will say, since you have known him—though I remember him, just after his marriage, poor fellow, full of hope and joy; but of late his melancholy has deepened. It has seemed to me as though he were always making an effort to throw off some monopolising thought. Has that struck *you*, Mr. Barlow?'

The lawyer shook his head.

'No: I have not noticed any deeper depression. He always seemed to me a disappointed man, and, if I may say so without offence, to have entertained, somewhat weakly, a sort of grudge against the general arrangements of the world in consequence. I am speaking very plainly.'

'No matter, sir; if ever there was a time for plain speech, it has come now,' returned Uncle Stephen. 'As to the "grudge," I have noticed that too, but only quite recently. His talk to me of late has been vehement against the unjust distribution of wealth, and of the harshness engendered by habits of luxury. I thought nothing of that; it is a poor man's privilege; and to one with Matthew's gifts and sense of justice, many things must have seemed hard. But, within the last few weeks, his prejudices have taken a more personal direction. The dislike he expressed for Lady Pargiter—who seems to be a most contemptible woman—was quite unworthy of him, and, curiously enough, this seemed to extend to her inanimate possessions—I refer to her diamonds.'

The lawyer bowed his head; he was at

tentive enough to what his companion said, but had no notion whither he was driving.

'The diamonds, you see,' continued Uncle Stephen, with the air of one who talks and reflects at the same time, 'have been the immediate cause of much inconvenience and worry to him; they took him from his home of nights, and exposed him to humiliations, and—as I have since learnt—even to insults. How strange it seems that a few sparkling stones, which only served to make more hideous the woman that owned them, should be the cause of such trouble; stones that might have been turned to bread, or, in worthier hands, have realised the dreams of science!'

'But, excuse me, Mr. Durham, that will not hold water,' interrupted the lawyer. 'When that comes to be tried, it means crack-brained socialism—mere madness.'

'Just so: yet those words, which I have purposely addressed to you as my own, Matthew Helston spoke to me the very night on which he disappeared from us. In my opinion, as in yours, it seems, they were mere madness.'

'Good Heavens! do you think he was mad?'

'Of course I should not have thought so had nothing come of it; indeed, as it was, I remember rallying him upon his strange opinions: "If Mr. Signet knew them," I said, "he would be afraid of your dropping those diamonds into the river." And then he answered what I think has now great significance. "No; if I took them, I should certainly not enrich Father Thames with them"—implying, of course, that he would take them for himself.'

'To "realise the dreams of science," observed Mr. Barlow, in a hushed voice; 'that is, to furnish the funds for the prosecution of his invention, I suppose. I am afraid a jury——'

'Never mind the juries just now, Mr. Barlow: nevertheless, what you suggest is possible. Poor Madge was no doubt another disturbing element with him; but mainly it was the jewels. My theory (of course it is nothing more, but it has the advantage of explaining *everything*) is that, through dwelling almost exclusively upon this single subject, Matthew's mind became unhinged. Of course there has been method in his madness; he *did* return to Lady Pargiter's (she has lied about that, it seems, and been found out) and afterwards dismissed the cabman with the pretence that he was going to remain in Moor Street. Then, under the influence of his monomania, he took away the diamonds.'

'It is possible,' mused the lawyer. 'I have known cases quite as black where we have pulled the man through. There is nothing like kleptomania for bamboozling a jury.'

'Good Heavens, sir, will you keep your mind clear of juries!' exclaimed Uncle Stephen impatiently. 'For my part, I would as soon have diamonds on the brain as twelve men in a box. The mania I speak of has no more to do with kleptomania than has a horse-chestnut with a chestnut horse. It is a mental aberration—analogous to sleep-walking — caused by allowing the thoughts to dwell upon one topic, and those depressed by melancholy are especially subject to it. That is my view of Matthew's case. It explains all that can be explained, and it contains this comfort in it—such aberrations are temporary ; so Matthew may yet be restored to us and in his right mind.'

It was on the tip of Mr. Barlow's tongue to say, 'And the diamonds?' But he thought it might suggest juries, and cause another outbreak : moreover, he had a high opinion of Mr. Durham's intelligence as a psychologist, and thought his theory worth attention.

It was noteworthy that this opinion of Mr. Durham's was the first expression of a doubt from the side of Matthew's friends, not indeed of his innocence, but of his absolute disconnection with the Robbery in Moor Street.

CHAPTER XXXII.

MR. SIGNET HAS A BAD QUARTER OF AN HOUR.

ON Tuesday morning, when Mr. Signet arrived at his office, he found a business note
awaiting him, couched in studiously matter-
of-fact language.   It was written, to be sure,
on pink paper, and had a crest on it that
was meant to look as like a coronet as any
crest could be which was not one; but then,
that was the way in which Lady Pargiter's
business letters always arrived.

'Lady Pargiter begs to inform Mr. Signet
that she will require her diamonds on Thurs-
day evening next, at ten o'clock.'

This simple communication, of which he
had received scores before, worded almost
precisely in the same manner, almost took
the jeweller's breath away. If she had added
the postscript which she sometimes did—

'Lady Pargiter requests that the person sent with the jewels will be punctual' (though Matthew was always in time), the communication could scarcely have more completely ignored all that had taken place since that fatal Friday.

Mr. Signet's impulse was to sit down and write a violent letter, assuring her ladyship that if her hypocrisy was intended to impose on him in any way, it was altogether thrown away; and hinting that if anybody, in *his* (Mr. Signet's) opinion, was more likely than another to know what had become of Mr. Helston and the jewels, it was Lady Pargiter herself; but he had the prudence to wait for Mr. Brail's arrival before committing himself to this step.

The detective, though by no means so much moved by her ladyship's letter as his employer had been, attached to it even a greater significance.

'I don't mind being in hot water, Mr. Signet,' he said. 'Strong language and hustling, and even a rough and tumble with an ugly customer, are quite in my line; but I must feel my feet wherever I go; this water is too *deep* for me, and 1 cannot pretend to advise you. You must call in a solicitor. Her ladyship has done so already, I'll take my oath of it.'

'How do you know that?'

'Lor' bless you, that note is not her writing—or leastways somebody guided her pen. You should have seen her the other day, when I had the honour to call upon her; she was more like a wild cat than a baronet's lady, and all because of these same jewels. If left to herself, she couldn't have written on the subject in this quiet style; no, she's writing under advice. "It is not your business," some lawyer has been saying to her, "whether Mr. Signet has the diamonds or not; you needn't be supposed to know anything about it. Just write, as usual, *I want them by such a date;* then see what he'll say." They don't want to strike the first blow, Mr. Signet.'

'I don't like lawyers,' said the jeweller.

'One generally finds when one employs them that the setting costs more than the stone. Moreover, they so contrive matters—with this and that legal proceeding, and their confounded phraseology, which I believe is written with the ink of the cuttle-fish, so that no one should be able to follow it—that the client loses sight of his own case when once committed to their keeping. For my part, I like to see where I'm going, not to be led like a blind man—to be run over by a waggon-load of steel rails, perhaps, after all.'

'That is a way the lawyers have, no doubt,' assented Mr. Brail coolly; 'still, I should send for Cripps.'

Cripps and Archdale were, as the detective was well aware, Messrs. Star and Signet's legal advisers. They dwelt in the East, and were thought to be wise men—after the fashion of the children of this world.

'The first thing Cripps will do,' urged the jeweller, 'is to put John Rutherford in gaol. He has come across so very few honest men in his lifetime that he scarcely believes in their existence.'

'His experience, however, is no better as regards the other sex,' argued Mr. Brail. 'He won't take it for granted that Lady Pargiter herself is the driven snow. He ain't like the rest of the human race, the natural enemy of a cabman; because, you see, his clients pay for his cabs.'

Perhaps Mr. Signet did not take this circumstance into sufficient account, or perhaps he had a secret suspicion that (except in his own eyes) the case against Lady Pargiter— so far, at all events, as it was affected by Mr. Rutherford's evidence—would appear a weak one; but for the present at least he declined to call in the services of his lawyer.

'No, Brail, I'd rather trust to you to catch her ladyship tripping. When you've put the salt upon her tail, it will be time enough to call in Cripps. I suppose we must take some notice of the woman's letter?'

'Of course, sir; not to do so would be to betray weakness, and yet we must not commit ourselves by putting pen to paper. My advice is that you call in Moor Street, and answer it by word of mouth.'

'Don't you think *you'd* better go, Brail ?'

'Well, if you're afraid of her ladyship,' returned the detective.

'Afraid ! What should I be afraid of ?' interrupted the jeweller, with a flush of colour that showed how the imputation had gone home. 'She can't snap my nose off.' Mr. Brail shook his head, but by no means in negation ; on the contrary, his face seemed to say—'I am not so sure of that.'

'You see, sir, it's my business to be snapped at,' said he presently ; 'and even if I were to lose my nose, it would be but the fortune of war. I have no sort of objection to go to Lady Pargiter's ; but what would be the good of it ? Her eyes are now open to the fact that I am in your employment ; she would not be so frank with me—though it is true she lied considerably even then— as upon the last occasion ; whereas to you—

as a principal, although her enemy—she would speak her mind.'

Mr. Signet did not look as if this prospect was very grateful to him; no doubt it was desirable to learn, if possible, what Lady Pargiter had in her mind, but to hear her speak it—or even a piece of it—was not a treat to look forward to. On his native heath—in the establishment in Paulet Street—Mr. Signet knew how to meet his enemy; but in Moor Street— among her ladyship's minions, or, still worse, alone with her, with uo help within call— he felt that he should be at a disadvantage. He could not be said to be in bodily fear— though, if he had really believed that she had made away with his representative, that might of course have been possible—but he was certainly much dismayed at the notion of a *tête-à-tête* with her.

'I suppose, if I went,' said Mr. Signet (for it was pleasant to him to feel that he had still the alternative of not going), 'my line would be to hear all she has to say, and to answer as little as possible.'

'Just so; only you must stick to your guns, you know.'

'Why, really, Brail, one would think you took me for a coward!' exclaimed the jeweller; he felt very indignant with his companion, and not the less so that he was conscious of a certain moisture upon his brow caused by his own secret misgivings.

'Not at all—not at all!' protested the detective; 'but I know the influence of women. The arguments of a lady of title in her own house have a certain—what shall I call it?—impetus.'

'Oh, hang her impetus!' returned the jeweller. 'She won't argue me out of 25,000*l.*—Well, well, I'll go myself, then, to Moor Street this afternoon.'

Mr. Brail replied, 'Very good;' but there was a twitching at the corners of his mouth which betrayed that he was amused. He believed that his employer had fixed the afternoon instead of the morning for his visit, in hopes that he might find Lady Pargiter not at home.

If this had been Mr. Signet's expectation, it was doomed to disappointment. He timed his call (which certainly gave some colour to Mr. Brail's view) at an hour when a lady of fashion is almost certain to be visiting her acquaintances; but his inquiry as to whether her ladyship was within was answered in the affirmative, and he was shown up at once into her boudoir. He had been to Moor Street before, and he felt that there was a difference in the mode of his present reception. He could not be aware, of course, of what was actually the case, that her ladyship had been waiting for him with impatience throughout the day, and had given orders that no one else was to be admitted to her presence; but when he heard the front door clang behind him, he felt that he would have given five pounds to be on the other side of it. Nor did he like being ushered past the usual reception rooms to her ladyship's sanctum on the second floor.

She was sitting at her escritoire when he

entered the room, writing—or pretending to write—a letter.

She bowed and pointed to a chair, and for a few moments continued her occupation. Whether her doing so was an intentional impertinence or not, its effect was unfortunate for her; for it gave Mr. Signet time to collect his ideas, and—to say truth—to still a certain fluttering in the region of his heart, caused by the thought that his duel with this formidable antagonist, and on which so much depended, was about to begin.

'You got my note, I conclude, this morning, Mr. Signet?' she presently observed, with some abruptness.

'Yes, Lady Pargiter; I am here in consequence of it.'

She lifted her eyebrows, or rather (for she had none to lift) the skin of her forehead. She intended to signify, in an indifferent way—'Why have you taken so much trouble? A post-card would have done as well.' But her eyes belied her would-be careless look; they were fierce and wolfish.

'I thought, my lady, your communication a very extraordinary one, considering the circumstances of the case.'

'My communication?' Here her brow came down instead of up, in spite of herself. ' Do you mean my note?'

'Yes, madam. You cannot but be aware that your diamonds are not at present in my possession.'

'You are very much mistaken, Mr. Signet, for I believe they are.' The insult, and its suggestion, were unmistakable. Mr. Signet's swarthy face turned pale, and he did not answer her for some moments.

'I should have thought, madam, that you could scarcely have been ignorant,' he said, speaking very slowly, 'that since Friday morning last, when Mr. Helston called on you by appointment as usual, he has mysteriously disappeared.'

'I have heard something of that;— yes—' (she affected to consider)—' there was a paragraph about it in one of the papers.'

'And a policeman called here also, I

understood,' suggested Mr. Signet; his voice was low, but very clear: Lady Pargiter was still studiously indifferent. It was like the slow scrape of the rapiers before the quick thrust and parry.

'Yes: I saw him. He told me, as you say, that your confidential agent was missing. I was sorry for you, of course, but I did not think it necessary to condole with you in my note; it was only a letter of business, to tell you that I should want my diamonds on Friday.'

' Still, as the man was lost in your service, Lady Pargiter, as much as in my own, and more, one would have thought you would have alluded to it, unless you had reasons to the contrary. His disappearance has afflicted his unhappy wife and family beyond expression.'

'So I read in the newspaper, Mr. Signet. Still, as I had not the pleasure of their acquaintance, I did not condole with *them.* —Perhaps you have come about some sub-scription for them; if so, I must decline my

aid to any such purpose. Mr. Helston was
in your service—as to his being in mine, if
I had had any voice in the matter, which I
had not, I should have preferred some one
else ; you knew his worth, it seems ; *I*
didn't ; and of course it is to you his family
must look for recompense.'

'You take a hard view of the case, Lady
Pargiter.'

'Hard? I take no view of the case at
all, Mr. Signet ! Pray let us have done with
Mr. Helston.'

'And yet you must know that with Mr.
Helston your diamonds have also disappeared ? '

'I may know it, or believe it, from
report ; but I have no official information—
that is, from yourself—about it. In any
case, however, the matter does not concern
me. When I say I want my diamonds on
Friday, that means I must either have
them or their equivalent. The precise sum
agreed upon in our memorandum—I have

a duplicate of it somewhere—was, I think, 25,000*l.*'

'Then even while this affair remains a mystery, and Mr. Helston (whom I believe to be as innocent as your ladyship in this matter) is still only under suspicion, you would press for what you deem your legal rights?'

'Most certainly I shall do so.'

'Perhaps you have not considered, Lady Pargiter, that the very fact of my allowing your claim at this stage of the matter—supposing that I did so—would brand by implication Mr. Matthew Helston as a thief.'

'I have certainly not considered that, Mr. Signet; it is a contingency that has never entered into my thoughts; nor does it affect me now one feather's weight. You are taking up my time, sir, to no purpose. On Friday next—as I wrote to you—I demand of you either my diamonds or your money. I have nothing more to say.'

She half turned to her desk as if to

resume her writing, but he noticed that she still watched him—and with anxiety, too—from the corner of her eye.

'My diamonds or your money!' he repeated to himself fiercely. 'Why, this woman is like a highwayman with his "Your money or your life." Nay, she *is* a highwayman; a robber—for aught I know, a murderer. I will never pay her a sixpence.'

Then he answered, with quiet distinctness as before : 'You urge your claim with great severity, madam ; with a harshness, indeed, that reminds me of Shylock.'

'Of *whom*?' inquired Lady Pargiter, who, perhaps fortunately for the jeweller, was not a student of Shakespeare.

'Well, I will rather say, you remind me of your father, madam, in his strict adhesion to his legal claims. He would always have his bond—and so shall you. The strict letter of it, and not an iota more.'

'I don't want any more than 25,000*l.*, Mr. Signet,' replied the other coldly ; 'that is, if it is paid by Friday ; after that date I shall require the interest at five per cent. I think that was mentioned in the memorandum?'

'It was, Lady Pargiter. I have been refreshing my memory with that document this morning. It especially makes me responsible for the jewels in the person of my agent, whose receipt——'

He paused here by design. The boudoir was at the back of the house, removed from all noise and movement; there were but three things that struck upon his ear, as he spoke that pregnant word—the beating of his own heart; the ticking of the French clock upon the mantelpiece ; and the breathing of Lady Pargiter—which had suddenly become hard and loud: in her intense excitement, that equine peculiarity she had of 'snorting' had been involuntarily developed : her eyes had grown unnaturally prominent. Mr. Signet felt certain that the waiting-maid's information was to be relied on.

'In the person of my agent, whose receipt,' continued he, with great distinctness, 'shall be considered a full discharge of all responsibility on the part of Lady Pargiter —you hold that receipt, of course, my lady?'

For the moment he thought she would have struck him, and drew back mechanically. As she stretched out her long scraggy neck, and beaked face, with its purple flush, it reminded him of some angry vulture in the Zoological Gardens. 'You scoundrel!' she shrieked; 'you thief!'

'Ah, you have not got it, then,' said Mr. Signet, his triumph overpowering his fears. 'If you had, it would have been no matter. I have the cabman's evidence that my agent remained here, and your own disproved falsehood about sending your footman after him, to back it. I should therefore have declined to pay forfeit to you in any case; but now—now that I know you have not got the receipt—I will never pay you one penny. You want your legal rights, do you? you shall have them; try them, claim them, push them—and see what comes of it!'

If Lady Pargiter looked like a vulture, it should be added in fairness that her antagonist resembled a cockatoo: every word he uttered was delivered with a jerk of his head and body, to signify at once both victory and defiance. There was little wanting, in fact, to his similitude to the bird except the crest, and this he in part supplied by clapping his hat on in her ladyship's presence, and toddling rapidly from the room.

Not, however, before Lady Pargiter's voice reached him, laden with menace as well as reproaches.

'Cheat, thief, liar!' she cried, 'you have suborned my waiting-maid; but it shall not avail you. To-morrow—see what I will do to-morrow; look in the paper to-morrow morning, Mr. Signet.' And then again came her 'Cheat, thief, liar!' like the refrain of some cadger's song in a new 'Beggars' Opera.'

CHAPTER XXXIII.

TROUBLE IN THE MEWS.

NEXT to his friends in Cavendish Grove, there was no one in all London cognisant of Matthew Helston's disappearance—and who, by this time, but was aware of it?—who was half so much distressed by it as Mrs. Rutherford of Hybla Mews. She was grieved upon the missing man's account, distressed beyond measure upon that of his wife, and anxious and worried and indignant upon that of her husband. She was confident that he was as innocent of complicity with any crime—and especially one that had Matthew Helston for its victim—as one of his own cab-horses, but she could not conceal from herself that the circumstances of the case threw suspicion upon him. She admitted in her own mind that not only the

, visits paid to them by Miss Thurlow and Mr. Signet were only what might have been looked for, but that that even of Mr. Brail had been justified. This had not been her husband's view. In spite of the detective's earnest and confidential tone, honest John had known him to be a policeman—'spotted him,' as he had expressed it—at the first glance; and he had shown himself curt, not to say antagonistic, accordingly. It is one of the peculiarities of his class, when unjustly submitted to the examination of the civil power, to be so, and his morose behaviour had impressed Mr. Brail in his favour much more than if he had been fawning or even civil. Moreover, he had stuck precisely to the same tale throughout, which also worked in his favour, though cautious Mr. Brail by no means considered this conclusive: 'It might be or it mightn't,' he said; 'some folks blush because they're innocent, and others because they're guilty; some look you in the face because they have nothing to fear, and others because they're " owdacious." And just in the same way some will, stick to the same tale because it's true, and others because they have learnt it by heart —and when it was so, the shorter it was the better.' If John Rutherford had learnt his story by heart, he had learnt it very well. The hour he reached Moor Street with his fare; the hour he departed from it without him; the distance, as he judged, he had gone down the street before he was run after and recalled by 'Six-foot'; the space of time (a very short one) that had elapsed between Matthew's leaving the cab the usual time, and the message brought to him that his fare had been asked to stay, and the words of the message—all this never varied with him. 'It is the simple truth,' he would generally add, in a quiet, natural manner, which, when wearied by questioners (for everybody was curious to hear his story), he would supplement in this way: 'But if you don't choose to believe it, you may let it alone.' To the wife of his bosom he had said again and again, 'They may put me in prison, Sally, or they may cut my head off; but they won't get nothing more out of me.' And to her mind his words had carried conviction. But simple as she was, and ignorant of the ways of the great world, she knew more about those of ordinary life than Lady Pargiter; from the moment that Amy came with her sad news, she felt that Mr. Matthew Helston's case—especially as it included the Pargiter diamonds—was an egg to be hatched, if hatched at all, by a sitting magistrate; and that the person in whose company Mr. Helston had last been seen would be the person held responsible for his recovery.

Honest John, on the other hand, having given his testimony and expressed his willingness to give it again, appeared to feel no apprehensions on his own account, and ignored, or affected to ignore, all further responsibility. He was sorry, he said, very sorry, for Master Matthew, and most sincerely hoped all would turn out to be well with him; but if it were not well, he seemed to see no reason why it should be ill with himself. He went about his work as usual, and as if nothing had happened. Sally's love, however, quickened her fears, and made her observant. She saw that the cloud which hung over the missing man threw the shadow of suspicion, in their neighbours' eyes, over her husband, and that, though his society was much sought after in the Mews, and especially at the 'Rising Sun,' it was not out of friendship, but from a morbid curiosity. They liked to hear the details of his story, but especially from his own lips, because they felt he could tell so much more if he chose. This made her sad and very indignant, but not so much so as to forget the case of her good friend Mrs. Helston, who had so much more cause for sorrow—and indeed for indignation too—than she. The cabman's wife had a kind disposition and a mind not altogether uncultivated, and though she had been a domestic servant, she took none of that pleasure in family catastrophes which is an attribute—though by no means a peculiar

one—of her class. For the first few days
she had 'not the heart' to go to poor 'Miss
Sabey that was,' and condole with her upon
her great calamity; she had hoped, every
hour, that something would occur to clear
up the mystery of Mr. Helston's absence, and
to absolve her from so unpleasant an errand;
but she now began to feel that this duty was
incumbent on her, and ought to be no longer
delayed.

On the afternoon of Mr. Signet's visit to
Moor Street she accordingly walked over to
Cavendish Grove, and was received by Amy
very kindly.

'Whether my sister will feel able to see
you or not, I cannot say, Mrs. Rutherford.
In any case, I am sure she will take your
coming as very kind.'

'Don't speak of that, Miss Amy: of
course I understand what my presence must
remind her of; and if it's better not——'

'No, it is not that, Sally. There is no
fear of reminding my poor sister of what
never escapes her recollection even for an

instant. But, she may not feel equal to it.'

'I would not overtask her strength for worlds,' returned Sally gravely; 'if that is your real reason, it is sufficient for me. But you was never good at deceiving folks, Miss Amy: you could allus easier say " No," however it grieved you, and I do think you have some other objection in your mind. Perhaps Mrs. Helston thinks—God forgive her if it be so—that my John has some hand in her present calamity?'

'Heaven forbid!' replied Amy earnestly : ' no, pray don't think that, Sally.' Her hesitation had been caused, not indeed exactly as Mrs. Rutherford suggested, but by the opinions she had heard Frank express respecting the cabman; she herself believed in his innocence, but if her lover should happen to be right, how dreadful it would be for her sister to see this woman !

In the end she left the decision to Sabey herself, who was aware of Mr. Barlow's views. 'Of course I will see Sally,' was her sister's reply ; and the interview took place accordingly.

At the sight of Mrs. Helston, so white and wan, and 'with all the life taken out of her,' as her visitor afterwards expressed it, Mrs. Rutherford burst into tears.

'Don't cry, Sally,' said Sabey, putting up her thin cheek to the other's kiss; 'though indeed I wish I could weep as you do.'

'Indeed, Miss Sabey, I wish you could; for it always does one a power of good. And yet it is a good sign in your case, for if you thought Mr. Helston were really gone from you for ever, your tears would come quick enough.'

Sabey shook her head : she did think he was gone for ever, but she could not be sure.

'What a kind gentleman he was,' continued the good woman; 'and how considerate ! John says he never drove a fare like him : with always a pleasant word, or a bit of bacca, or a drop of good drink on a cold night. Even if it hadn't been Master Matthew, as he had known from a child, he'd 'a' took to him, he says, as he never took to anyone else.'

'If my husband missed his opportunities as people say,' said Sabey, as if speaking to herself, ' it was not those which were offered to him of doing a kindness to his fellow-creatures.'

'That is very true, ma'am; he could never hurt a fly; and to think that anybody would have done harm to him for the sake of them rubbishy diamonds, is almost past belief.'

'There are very wicked people in the world, I fear,' said Amy.

'Yes, and some as has no call to it, as you may say, ma'am: folks out of the reach of temptation, like Lady Pargiter.'

'Let us speak ill of no one without proof,' said Sabey solemnly. She had not, as we know, been wont to spare her ladyship, for had not her Matthew had good cause for disliking her? but of late Sabey had

altered in this respect : if her husband were
dead, it seemed a want of reverence to his
memory to keep alive anything (such as a
prejudice or animosity) that might now
appear to eyes from which the scales had
fallen an unworthiness. Moreover, Sabey,
who had thought the whole matter out a
hundred times, did not believe in Lady Pargiter's guilt; and was it not her duty to
reprove slander, which was even now flicker-
ing with its forked tongue against her own
dearest and nearest !

'I don't know about proof,' said Mrs.
Rutherford : 'but the mistress of them in
whose company he was seen last—and they
were Lady Pargiter's servants—ought to
know more about what has become of your
poor husband than anyone else.'

There was no answer. Amy kept her
eyes upon the ground, and Sabey was looking
straight before her in semi-unconsciousness
of her visitor's presence. To her the woman's
words, though they had a direct reference to
her bereavement, scarcely reached her sense :

she was like one who, full of thought and years, listens to the voice of some young pulpiteer preaching upon 'Fate, Freewill, Foreknowledge absolute;' the topic is important, but from him no new light is likely to be shed upon it.

'You think my John a liar?' said Mrs. Rutherford suddenly.

'Indeed, Sally, we don't say that,' observed Amy gently.

'But you think it, and Mrs. Helston thinks it.'

'The night was dark,' said Sabey, with grave distinctness, like a judge who is giving his charge to a jury; 'the snow was falling and the wind was blowing. Your husband was tired, no doubt; his senses were not so keen as under other circumstances; and he may have been mistaken as to what was said to him by the footman regarding my dear husband.'

'It was not so, Miss Sabey; indeed it was not so. John had his senses about him quite as usual, and he had taken no liquor:

However, as you say, he may have been mistaken; but oh, my dear young ladies, he was not misguided. You have said just now that we should speak ill of no one without proof: but is it not as wrong to *think* ill of them? You are woe-stricken, dear Miss Sabey, and hardly answerable, perhaps, for the thoughts which sorrow has put into your heart: I forgive you them whatever they be. But do not think, I pray you do not think, that my John is to blame in this matter. His heart is as sound, ma'am, as your poor husband's is; and though he has done fewer kindnesses to others, he is mindful of those which have been done to him. If I thought that John, my John, could so far forget whose wife it was who came to me in the fever as to lift his hand——'

'Sally, Sally, we don't think it,' expostulated Amy, for the woman had thrown herself upon her knees, in a passion of mingled repudiation and appeal.

'You do—*she* does!' cried Sally. 'She thinks my husband has robbed, perhaps murdered, his friend and benefactor. If I thought so, so help me Heaven, I would give him up to the hangman with my own hands.'

'Sally—Sally—forgive me,' faltered Sabey, rising from her chair, and holding out her arms for her embrace. 'If I have done your husband wrong in thought—and perhaps I have—I humbly ask your pardon. The best, the most honest of us (alas! I know it) do not, where all is dark, escape suspicion. I know, as well as He who made him, that my Matthew is as pure as snow from the least stain upon his honour. I loathe, despise, abhor those who dare to hint otherwise. Then, why should I deny to you the faith that I hold so firmly in my own case? I do not deny it, Sally. I believe your husband to be innocent of all complicity in this matter; that he has had no hand whatever in breaking this poor heart.'

'The Lord Almighty bless you and comfort you, Miss Sabey, for saying those blessed words,' sobbed the good woman. 'Oh, how glad I am I came to you!'

It was strange to see—and might have been a lesson to the most melancholy—what joy had been imparted to this good woman by poor Sabey, who herself was absolutely joyless.

Mrs. Rutherford returned home that afternoon a far happier woman, for it had weighed heavily on her mind that Mrs. Helston might entertain bitter thoughts of her John. All she had said in his defence to her had been genuine and honest. Only, in order to introduce the subject, she had spoken out more plainly against Lady Pargiter—and had been very properly reproved for it—than she had been justified in doing; for in her heart of hearts she did not believe that her ladyship had had any hand in the matter. Her husband thought otherwise, it was true, and his evidence, in which she believed in every particular, tended that way, no doubt; but she herself felt that there must be some mistake. Her ladyship's servants—some of those good-for-nothing 'Six-feet'—might have done the mischief among themselves; but she could not believe that Lady Pargiter had stolen her own diamonds.

That other persons, such as Captain Langton, had had their eye upon them, she was satisfied, and on them her suspicions would have rested, but for the fact that it was under Lady Pargiter's roof that Matthew was left by her husband, and that out of Lady Pargiter's doors he had never since been seen to pass.

On her returning home, she was disappointed at finding that John had not yet returned, for she longed to tell him that she had been to Cavendish Grove, and made his peace for him with Mrs. Helston; in her state of mental excitement, she found she could not sit down as usual to her needlework; her thoughts were always straying to the poor forlorn young lady she had just left, and to the mysterious calamity that had befallen her. 'I can't stand this,' she murmured to herself at last; 'I shall go mad, if

I keep thinking about it, without a soul to talk to.   I'll just run up and down the walls, and put things straight.'

To an ordinary intelligence her expressed intention of 'running up and down the walls' would have sounded as if Mrs. Rutherford were mad already; but it was a common term of hers for clearing out the premises and making them tidy: which occupation had such a charm for her (as it has with all good housewives) that when engaged in it she had no thoughts for anything else.   She did not possess that blessing to housemaids a Turk's-head broom, nor even a pair of steps, but mounting on a chair, she began to use a handbrush in a very workmanlike style. The room was low, so that even the ceiling was within reach of her ministrations: and very soon, not a cobweb nor a speck of dust was to be seen.   She was just giving a finishing touch to the top of their common wardrobe, which was however out of sight, when her brush knocked against some metallic substance.   'Lawk a mercy, why, what's that?' cried Sally. She put up her hand with no little curiosity, and from the receptacle in question, where it had evidently been placed for the purpose of concealment, she brought out a large pistol. Amazement and alarm were at first her only feelings : she had a belief in the danger of firearms which unhappily is not always found coexistent with an ignorance of their use, and she laid the weapon upon the table, taking care to point the muzzle away from her, as though it had been a self-acting Infernal Machine. When it showed no signs of going off, her personal apprehensions subsided, but only to be replaced by fears of another kind. How on earth had her husband come to be possessed of such an instrument? What did a cabman want with a pistol? Even if she had known it was a horse-pistol, it would have been no answer to such a question; as it was, there was not a trace of association between them. It had felt so heavy that she was convinced that it was loaded; but, loaded or not, what business had her John

What did a cabman want with a pistol?

to own it? That it was his she had no
doubt; for she had known him to use the
top of the wardrobe before for purposes, as
he flattered himself, of concealment; being
under the impression that her brush did not
invade that dust-covered but elevated region.
Now, with pistols Sally was always accustomed to associate crimes of violence: and
had not such a crime been in all probability
committed upon Mr. Matthew Helston? The
inference was only too obvious. She did not
even now think her husband guilty of an
offence so heinous, but she did not feel that
certainty of his innocence which she had
entertained five minutes ago. Suppose the
police had been sent by Mr. Brail or Mr.
Signet to search the room? If she had not
found the pistol, most certainly they would
have done so, and drawn the worst deduction
from it. The very idea of such a thing made
her stout limbs quake with fear. Her first
thought was how to get rid of it, or at all
events to place it in some more secret spot.
She thought for a moment of putting it into

the fire, but, fortunately for her nerves, gave up that plan; she reflected that iron did not easily melt. Then another element suggested itself, which would hide the thing equally well, and also have the advantage of quenching its powers for ill. With infinite caution, she lifted the pistol, as she afterwards described it, ' by the ears '—it was fortunately at half-cock, or the hammers might have resented this treatment—and stepping into the verandah, dropped it gently into the water-butt below.

Then she awaited the return of her husband, with anxiety indeed and misgivings, but with somewhat less of immediate alarm. The good news she had had to give him had vanished: it was no longer in her mind; and what sort of news, she wondered, would John, under compulsion, have to give her? That he had concealed something from her, besides the pistol, was certain: the only question now was, How much? or How bad?

CHAPTER XXXIV.

ANOTHER DESERTER.

It has been cruelly and falsely said (generally in excuse for some harsh conduct or neglect upon our own parts towards them) that the poor do not feel so acutely as their betters; that domestic calamities fall lighter on them; and that even disease does not wring them with such pain as it causes more tenderly nurtured bodies. The explanation for this fallacy probably lies in the fact that their troubles are so severe that ordinary woes seem by comparison insignificant to them; a toothache that makes *us* doubt the benevolence of the scheme of creation is to them a toothache and nothing more; and happy are they if they possess the shilling that absolves them from the kind offices of an amateur tooth-drawer; while to the rheumatism whose pangs we resent so bitterly, the field labourer's back is bowed in patient acquiescence, as to an ill to which his class is heir. On the other hand, it is certain that the poor are not easily affected by mental anxiety : a fortunate thing for those whose livelihood so often depends on the caprice of a master. The carelessness with which the domestic servant will leave her 'place,' the readiness with which the workman will throw up his employment, and trust to the chapter of accidents for a new situation, are marvellous. Risks do not appal them; misfortune, as a rule, throws no shadow upon them until it is actually at their doors.

Hence it was that, though Mr. John Rutherford could not but be aware that he was looked upon with public suspicion in reference to Mr. Helston's disappearance and the missing diamonds, and might any day find himself in 'Queer Street' in consequence, the circumstance did not much disturb his equanimity. Nor was he so much distressed upon Master Matthew's account as his wife would have preferred to see him.

'*He'*ll come out of it all right, sooner or later, old woman,' he was wont to reply to Sally's often expressed fears; and this confidence on his part had been wont to afford her some consolation. What she had understood him to mean was that though, in his view, Lady Pargiter had put Matthew out of the way for the time, in order to dispose of the jewels in security, she was by no means likely to proceed to the last extremity and murder him.

But when her husband returned that evening, after her discovery of the pistol, and as usual in very tolerable spirits, all her former surmises were put to the rout. She felt comfort in nothing, and sure of nothing except that his lively whistling gave her extreme annoyance, for it seemed to her a sign of callousness.

'You are very gay, John,' she said with significance, ' but if you had been with me to-day, and seen how poor Mrs. Helston was looking, it would have sobered you.'

'Sobered me?' returned her husband; 'so help me Bob, I have touched nothing but beer—and only a pint of that—the livelong day.'

'Oh, I don't mean drink; and it's my belief you know well enough that I don't, John; it's your reckless devil-may-care way of going on that shocks *me*.'

'Well, you mentioned drink, Sally,' replied the cabman, to all appearance in genuine astonishment, 'and hang me if I don't think you've been at the gin-bottle. Because Master Matthew has been kidnapped (for that's what's happened, I'll bet a shiner), and his missus is naturally cut up about it, is it therefore a sin for me to whistle?'

'The sin ain't in the whistling,' replied his lady darkly. 'A man sometimes whistles to hide the remorse as is a-gnawing of him.'

'Annoying of him?' replied honest John, for whom this eloquence was too highflying. 'To my mind, it's a deuced sight more

annoying than whistling to find black looks
and an empty supper-table when you come
home after a hard day's work.'

'You shall have your supper, John, directly,' said Sally, somewhat moved by this
reproof; albeit it was the first time she had
forgotten to prepare her husband's meal for
him, for many a day; 'though, for my part,
I wonder at some persons possessing an
appetite, with such a weight upon their
minds.'

'A weight? One would really suppose
I had got Mr. Matthew Helston in my pocket,'
exclaimed John, looking round on space
appealingly.

'I don't know *what* you've got in your
pocket, not I,' returned Mrs. Rutherford,
fixing him with her eye; 'perhaps another
loaded pistol.'

John's face did not easily turn colour—
exposure to the weather and pretty liberal
potations having made it tolerably 'fast'—
but through its ordinary hue of blue and red
'came a colour and a light, as I've seen the

·rosy red blushing in the northern night;' and at the same time his glance mechanically wandered to the top of the wardrobe.

'Oh yes: that's where it was,' cried Sally sardonically; 'and it's no use denying that you put it there. May I ask you, John Rutherford, what an honest cabman can want of loaded pistols?'

Notwithstanding that he was by nature somewhat garrulous, Mr. Rutherford kept silence for some moments; he scratched his huge and tangled head, his great body swayed from side to side in mental perturbation, and after all there came this *ridiculus mus* of a reply—

'You may ask, of course. There's no law agin asking, as I'm aweer on; but as to answering—well, I shan't, and that's flat.'

'You'll tell me, at all events, whether I've got a murderer for my husband?' inquired Sally, with solemnity.

'Well, not at present—no, you ain't,' replied John; 'though if you go on in that aggravating way,' he added with irritation, 'there's no knowing what you may drive me to.'

'It's conscience as is driving you, not me, and has got the whip-hand of you,' replied Sally. 'You may try to drown it in liquor——'

'A pint of beer,' interrupted John con temptuously.

'Or you may glaze it over with whistling and such like,' continued his lady; 'but your sin will find you out, John. To think that an honest man, as you once were, should have come to such a pass as to want loaded pistols !'

'Where is it ?' inquired John, in dicta-torial tones.

'Where you won't find it,' replied Sally defiantly; 'where the police won't find it, neither, I hope; for if they did, what would become of you, a man as they suspect al-ready ? Never will I sleep by your side agin, John, unless you tell me what you wanted with that pistol.'

'Then you must lie on the floor, Sally, for I never will.'

She knew by his tone that obstinacy had set in with him, and that all direct attempts to move him would be futile. If John had been a Cabinet Minister instead of a cabman, he would have been justly celebrated for an inflexible determination; as it was, he had the more humble reputation of being the most pigheaded man in Hybla Mews.

'Don't let's quarrel, John,' said Sally humbly. 'Whatever you've done, it is my duty to stick by you; but I think a wife—and a good one, such as I have been to you——'

He nodded with the gravity of a judge: so far the Court was with her.

'I think, I say, I have a right to your confidence. As it is, I don't even know how to defend you. Do you think I walked to Cavendish Grove to-day and back only to comfort poor dear Miss Sabey as was? No, John; it was also to clear your character in her eyes. And I thank Heaven I did it.

" Do you think my John," says I, " would have knowingly done any harm to Master Matthew ?" '

'That was right enough,' said John approvingly.

'Yes; but how can I feel that it was right enough *now* ? How can I lay my hand upon my heart, and say—" My husband is as innocent as the babe unborn," when I know he carries a loaded pistol ? Honest folks don't carry such things, but only thieves and murderers.'

'Then it's a pity you found it,' said John cunningly, and in a tone of satisfaction at his own logical acumen. 'The less you knows the better you seems to manage. I'm not agoing to tell you why I bought that there pistol, Sally; but I will tell you this much for your comfort—the use of it, whatever it was, is dead and gone. You may keep it for yourself—to shoot the beetles with—for all I care.'

'*I* keep it ! I wouldn't have such a thing in *my* house, far less my hand—for its weight in gold.   I've throwed it into the water-butt.'

'Don't you think it'll give rather a taste to the tea?' suggested Mr. Rutherford. 'Iron, they say, is strengthening to the system; but I am not so sure about powder and lead.'

'Then it *was* loaded, John?' said Sally despondingly.

'Well, yes, it was; but I'll say this much—and mind you, it's the very last I *will* say—that pistol was not meant to do any harm to Master Matthew. Quite the contrary.'

'I thank Heaven for that, John!' exclaimed Sally with genuine satisfaction. But the next moment her brow became clouded. She wished to ask him a certain question which she could not muster courage to put into words.

'I think you had better fish that pistol out,' he said suddenly, 'and then throw it away somewhere. As you say, if the Police found it, it might bring someone into trouble.'

Sally did not ask who the someone was, but instantly took up the tongs and went out on the verandah. The night had fallen by that time, and no one standing in the Mews could have seen what she was about. Nevertheless, there was a star or two, the light of which was sufficient to indicate the surface of the water—only it did not do so. Sally knew, however, where to find the butt; and, kneeling on the wooden gallery, thrust down the tongs in the direction of it. But they only struck against its wooden walls.

'Why, the water has leaked out, John,' she whispered in a frightened tone. 'That's a strange thing.'

'It would be much stranger if the pistol had flowed through the spigot,' answered John, with the air of one who understands practical science. 'There's a ladder agen the butt below——' But Sally had already run downstairs to carry out the suggested plan. She was longer away than could be accounted for by the nature of her errand, and when she came back her look of alarm had turned to one of positive terror.

'The pistol's gone, John!'

'What d'ye mean?' he said. 'Gone off of itself, and in a butt of water!'

'No; the spigot's out. Some one has drawed off the water, and taken away the pistol.'

'Whew!' Though written as a monosyllable, this word was prolonged in Mr. Rutherford's lips to a quite extraordinary extent, and his face wore a very serious expression as he uttered it. 'The Perleece have been at their little games,' he murmured. 'Well, let 'em. He must be out of harm's way by this time.'

'*Who* must be out of harm's way?' inquired Sally quickly.

'Never you mind,' he answered gruffly; 'you've meddled enough already for one day. If you hadn't found that there pistol the Perleece would not have found it. Can't you leave things alone ? Let's have supper, will you. If you say another word about the pistol or Master Matthew, I'm off to the " Rising Sun." '

There was nothing Mrs. Rutherford disliked more than her husband leaving her for the public-house; and just now, of all times, it was terrible to her to have him out of her sight: so she proceeded to lay the supper-table without a word. She now felt certain that he had compromised himself in the Moor Street affair, but no longer feared that he had done harm to Mr. Helston. He had said that that pistol was bought, not to harm him, but 'quite the contrary.' Now, 'quite the contrary' could only mean to help him—to further some scheme of Mr. Helston's own. Moreover, to whom could he have referred but to Mr. Helston when he had muttered to himself—'He must be out of harm's way by this time'? Her husband was no murderer, and perhaps no thief in any personal sense; but she knew how strong were his likes and dislikes—his notions of sticking to his friends, and never betraying them ; and in spite of herself she now entertained a dreadful apprehension that he had been playing into his friend and employer's hands.

And thus of the faithful few that still believed in Matthew Helston's innocence as respected the Pargiter diamonds, one more had gone over—if not to the Enemy, to the Majority.

CHAPTER XXXV.

THE POSTHUMOUS LETTER.

READER, has it ever fallen to your duty to open the desk of one very dear to you, and who is dead, and to suffer anew the parting with him at the sight of every 'trivial fond record'? There is scarcely one of all the sad experiences to which human nature is heir, more pathetic, more heart-breaking. His handwriting lies before you, with his thoughts still living in it, though the fingers that set them down are cold in death. Here is a faded flower, memorial of you know not what, but doubtless of some tender time; its blossom has withered, its stalk is dry, but it has not yet become dust as he has. There are letters from others, tied round with loving care, and doubtless intended to be read again by eyes to whom the page of

Futurity alone is now open.   Perhaps one of
your own letters is among them—let us hope
a kind one—how strangely has it altered to
your view ; it is no longer a mere vehicle of
your own feelings, but has become a material
link with the other world !

On such a bitter task, on Friday, December 18, exactly one week after her
husband's disappearance, Mrs. Helston was
engaged. She was not certain, it is true,
that her Matthew was dead; she wore no
outward mark of the widow about her—save
in the wan cheek and the hollow eye—but
her heart was almost as hopeless and forlorn
as though she had been one. She had undertaken this sad office under the combined
advice of Uncle Stephen and Mr. Barlow ;
not that they expected ought to come of it,
but because it was just possible—in the absence of all other explanations of the enigma
—that some clue to the mystery of her husband's absence might be discovered among
his own documents. The very suggestion, as
they were well aware, had the elements of

suspicion or disparagement about it; but that, as they foresaw, never entered into Sabey's mind. They had put it to her in this way :—'It is possible, just possible, that Matthew has come to harm at the hand of some private enemy. So far as we know, it is true, he had none; nay, he himself may have been unaware of the existence of such a person, and yet it may be otherwise. We think that every private paper should be examined which may throw the least light upon his relations with other people.'

At first Sabey showed great unwillingness to accede to this proposal. It seemed to her irreverent, she said, thus to pry into her lost husband's private affairs, but her real reason was that the fact of her so doing seemed a tacit admission that he was lost to her for ever; it could affect the fact, of course, neither one way nor the other; but the feeling may well be excused, when we consider how many matter-of-fact and otherwise sensible persons object to make their wills. In the end, however, as we have said, she consented. One of the reasons that had weighed with her, in addition to the chief one, had been a certain argument of Mr. Barlow's :—

' In your case,' he had said, ' dear Sabey, there need be no apprehension of any record coming to light to pain you. Matthew's life was stainless.'

His use of the past tense made her lips quiver, but she only bowed her head. Of course Matthew's life had been stainless; but, if she refused to do their bidding, they might think perhaps that she entertained suspicions to the contrary: an idea that would certainly not have entered her head a week ago ; but now, with all the newspapers, and the world that read them, imputing evil to her husband, she had become sensitively jealous for his honour.

Matthew's desk was characteristic of its owner: a plain ink-stained affair with no conveniences within it such as shelves and drawers, but fastened by a good lock of his own making; the very taking of the key from its bunch was a sore trial to her, and, before putting it to its use, she cleaned it with a piece of leather—lest it should be rusted with her tears, she said to herself—but in reality to gain time. The contents of the desk were also characteristic. They consisted almost entirely of mathematical calculations; row after row of figures, the meaning of which was utterly unknown to her, but which she guessed, rightly, had reference to 'Madge.' They were all beautifully written out, and every paper appeared to be arranged with reference to the others. But, dear as had been his hopes in that direction, his heart—or at least the core of it—had lain elsewhere. Every letter—they were not many—she had ever written to him was found there, tied up in two packets. In one were those she had addressed to him as her lover, and dated from the Rectory; in the other the few she had had occasion, since their marriage, to write to him in Paulet Street—for they had never been separated by any longer distance.

'From dearest Sabey,' was inscribed on the former; and on the latter, 'From my darling wife.' It was terrible that the assurance of Love should inflict such cruel pangs. She opened one or two of them: they had not, of course, the power to move her as Matthew's own letters—sacred relics, stored in her own chamber, which she had not had the courage to touch—would have done; but nevertheless, in recalling the happy past, they shot sharp arrows into her heart. There was also a memorandum of the sums that had been expended by Mr. Durham in the promotion of Madge's interests, and a letter bound up with them by a plain india-rubber band, but sealed, addressed 'For Uncle Stephen, in case anything should happen to me.'

A strange addition under the circumstances enough, but which did not strike Sabey with much significance. She knew how deeply Matthew had felt his uncle's kindness, and she could easily conceive that gratitude had caused him to make this simple proviso for expressing itself to the good old man, in case opportunity should be otherwise denied him : the letter probably also bequeathed his wife and child to his uncle's care, albeit that might have seemed superfluous. To one who had known Matthew Helston less thoroughly, his leaving such a document behind him would have looked like a morbid presentiment of death, but to Sabey the incident was easily accountable.

Matthew had a horror of 'risks:' because Fortune perhaps had gone so ill with him, he had an objection to leave anything to chance; nor would he trust to the most natural contingencies, if it was possible for him to make a thing secure without them. And, moreover, he was always looking to the future. It was therefore without any foreboding as to its contents that Sabey took the letter from its receptacle, and, having wiped her tears, carried it into the next room, where Amy and Mr. Durham were sitting.

'Well, darling?' inquired the former, tenderly; she had left her sister alone with her sad task from motives of delicacy, but she read in her face how she had suffered in the ordeal. 'Have you found anything?'

Sabey shook her head. 'Only what I knew I should find. There is, however, this note for you, Uncle Stephen.'

'For me?' said the old man, reading the superscription: '*For Uncle Stephen, in case anything should happen to me.*'

'How strange!' exclaimed Amy, with excitement.

Mr. Durham was excited too, and being aware of the fact, he purposely delayed to open the envelope. He felt that presence of mind was necessary in case anything had to be concealed from Sabey.

'I can guess its contents,' said she softly. 'Matthew wishes to express to you in writing the thanks you would never listen to from his lips. The note was wrapped up with some memoranda of his money obligations to you. These he might have paid, had the chance been given him : his debt of gratitude never.'

'Poor fellow, dear fellow!' murmured Uncle Stephen. 'Yes; it is as you say. To his generous nature every little kindness loomed so large.'

Sabey could read what had been written to her husband's disparagement : such things turned her heart to steel. But she could not bear to hear him praised : that melted it. With a deep sob, she hurried from the room.

Amy was too wise to follow her immediately; and besides, something in the old man's manner had attracted her attention.

'Can I see that letter, Mr. Durham?'

'I had rather not show it you, my dear,' he answered quietly.

'If it really only contains dear Matthew's expression of his gratitude to you, I can picture it for myself. I know how he loved you.'

'It does contain something else, Amy. But it is only a matter of business.'

Then Amy gathered up her work, and withdrew to comfort Sabey.

Left alone, Mr. Durham took the letter from his pocket, and re-read it very carefully :—

'My dear Uncle Stephen,' it began,—'In case I should not live so long as the Tables of the *Phœnix'* [this was his life assurance company] 'have calculated, and you should survive me, I wish to add one more item to the long debt of gratitude I owe you. The sense of obligation, like other senses, is, I suppose, blunted by long use, or surely I should feel ashamed at asking any further favour of you. That the service I am about to ask of you must be a secret one—even from my wife, and indeed especially from her—will be an additional reason for your undertaking it; it is your delight, I know, to let your right hand know not what your left hand does for others ; the matter is also one of great delicacy, which will further recommend it to your noble nature. When I add that I entreat this kindness of you with my last breath, I feel that I need say no more.

' Please to pay to Lucy Matlock, a young woman at present residing at 80 Bleak Street, Bloomsbury, the sum of 10s. *weekly*, and if possible ensure the continuance of this allowance after your death. I have only one other favour to ask of you; that, for my sake, you will not seek to inquire into her story.—I am, dear Uncle Stephen, your loving and grateful nephew,

' MATTHEW HELSTON.'

END OF THE SECOND VOLUME.

LONDON : PRINTED BY
SPOTTISWOODE AND CO., NEW-STREET SQUARE
AND PARLIAMENT STREET

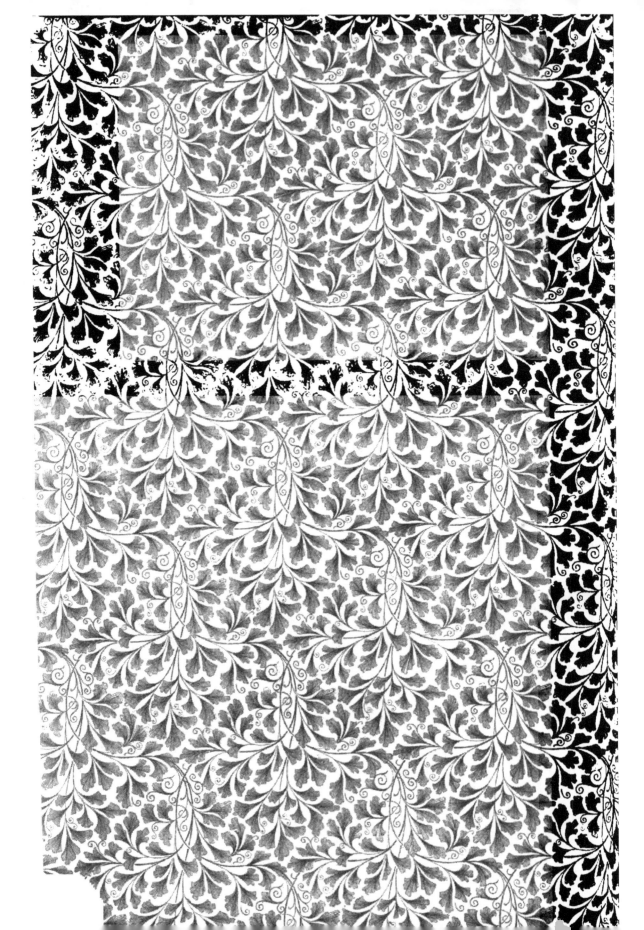

www.ingramcontent.com/pod-product-compliance
Lightning Source LLC
Chambersburg PA
CBHW080153060326
40689CB00018B/3960